Cybersecurity

Essential Guide for Beginners to Learn Basic Methods of Cybersecurity

HENRY GEORGE

TABLE OF CONTENTS

Introduction

Cybercrime is an international issue that has been dominating the electronic media circles for the last few years. It is a consistent threat targeting individuals as well as the big global companies, research institutes, and government departments. Cybercrimes in today's era have become more organized than the cybercrimes carried out by the lone hackers in the past. Nowadays, cybercriminals hire highly skilled developers and cybersecurity experts to exploit the cyber world. With a huge amount of exploitable data present online, cybersecurity has become indispensable.

The cybercriminals have developed sophisticated methods to target the cyber world. These cybercriminals can impact anyone using the internet which may include individuals, small enterprises, and large-scale organizations. Presently, most of the individuals, as well as the organizations, have understood the significance of cybersecurity. They are all focusing on taking all the potential measures to tackle cyber threats. Nowadays, cybercriminals and hackers are innovating novel techniques to breach the web-protocols. Therefore, the individuals and the organizations need to stay one step ahead to deal with the threats. As we wish to connect every gadget to the internet, it enhances the likelihood of vulnerabilities, flaws, and breaches. Those days are gone when mere passwords were sufficient to safeguard personal data. More advanced security is required to protect our data (either personal or professional). Therefore, adequate knowledge of cybersecurity is required by every individual to ensure data security from cyber-attacks.

We can define cybersecurity as a set of methods used to safeguard the integrity of data, networks, and programs from damage, attacks, and unauthorized access. Security can be classified into two sub-categories, i.e., physical security and cybersecurity. Both of these securities are essential to protect the computerized systems from unauthorized access. Therefore, most of the organizations focus on fortifying both aspects of security. Information security (a subset of cybersecurity) focusses on maintaining the confidentiality, integrity, and availability of personal or professional data. The implementation of cybersecurity and information security helps in preventing data breaches, identity thefts, and cyber-attacks.

This book offers an overview of essential components and methods of cybersecurity. The first three chapters of the book contain fundamental knowledge of cybersecurity, while the later chapters focus on different methods of cybersecurity. The knowledge of the internet and the underlying phenomena occurring in the cyber world is essential to understand the basics of cybersecurity. Chapter 1 briefly covers the introduction to the cyber world by discussing the fundamentals of internet technology. Moreover, three major components of cybersecurity (i.e., CIA triad) are also discussed in this chapter. Chapter 2 introduces the readers to the world of cybercrimes. Different categories of cybercrimes and hackers are discussed in the chapter.

Moreover, some tips regarding protection from cybercrimes are also discussed in the chapter. It is essential to understand the types of cyber-attacks to develop any cybersecurity solution. Chapter three focusses on the classification of typical cyber-attacks and security countermeasures to tackle them.

Different methods of cybersecurity have been develop to counter cyber-attacks. Chapter four briefly discusses different methods of cybersecurity. The remaining three chapters of the book are structured into individual, domain-specific topics. Readers can treat these chapters individually. However, novel cybersecurity techniques and topics discussed in these chapters are applicable to all domains discussed in other chapters of the book. Each chapter comprises an outline of a particular cybersecurity topic in a certain domain.

Chapter four introduces us to different types of cybersecurity methods. A brief description of the different tools and techniques used in cybersecurity are also discussed in Chapter four. Chapter five focuses on the detailed illustration of network security and cybersecurity of some critical infrastructures. Chapter 6 focusses on the methods of security testing to ensure the implementation of healthy cybersecurity systems. Chapter 7 deals with the fundamentals of web application security. Chapter 8 briefly discusses fundamental cybersecurity measures for reducing exploitable vulnerability and attacks.

Chapter 1

Introduction to Cyber World

Introduction

One of the most significant inventions of the 21st century is the internet, which has affected our lives to a great extent. Nowadays, the internet has crossed every obstruction and has altered the means we used to chat, work, play games, shop, listen to music, make friends, see movies, pay our bills, order food, greet our friend on their anniversaries or birthdays, etc. Applications have been developed to carry out most of the everyday tasks which has facilitated our life to a great deal by making it comfortable.

Contrary to the past, where one had to stand in a long queue for paying electricity and telephone bills; now, we can do that online through internet with a click of a button from our office or home. The technology has stretched to a level that we do not even need a computer for using the internet. We have smartphones equipped with internet, iPads, and palmtops, etc. using which we can keep in touch with our family, friends, and office throughout the day. Hence, the internet has not just simplified our life, but it has also provided a cost-effective solution to numerous problems.

Just a few years back, we used to make International Subscriber Dialing (ISD) calls or even a Subscriber trunk dialing (STD) calls, which were quite expensive. Both these methods were employed to deliver just critical messages, and the rest of the mundane communication was carried out through letters as it was a comparatively cheap mode of communication (Poe 2010). Today, we not only have the facility of making audio calls through internet but can also make video conference calls through various popular applications such as Skype, Viber, etc. at a very cheap expense to an extent where a 1-hour video call through internet is less costly than the rate of sending a 1-page document from New Jersey to California through a courier service. Not just this, the internet has also altered the way we used the typical devices. Now, besides watching our regular shows and movies on TV, we can use it for making calls, video chats with families and friends through the internet. Likewise, we can use our smartphones not just to make calls but also to watch any movie. Irrespective of our location, it is possible for us to keep in touch with the rest of the world. Working parents can keep an eye on their kids at home from the vicinity of their offices and can assist them in their homework. A businessman can easily keep an eye on his office, shop, workforce, etc. with a mere click of a button. It is safe to say that the internet has facilitated our life in numerous ways. Have you ever reflected on where this internet came from? Let us have a look at the brief history of the internet and learn how the internet was devised and how with time, it evolved to a level that it is now impossible for us to think of our lives without it.

History of the Internet

Interestingly, the foundation of the internet was laid as a result of the cold war between Russia and the USA. The world's first satellite SPUTNIK was launched into space by Russia on October 4, 1957. This was undoubtedly the success of Russia over the cyberspace and as a counteraction, in early 1960, the research agency of the Department of Defence, United States, namely, Advanced Research Projects Agency, affirmed the launch of ARPANET (Advanced Research Projects Agency NETwork). ARPANET was an experimental network and was developed to have the computers interconnected through this network so that they can communicate with one other even in case of emergencies such that in case of failure of any node owing to the bomb attack. The initial message was sent over the ARPANET from Leonard Kleinrock's laboratory located at the University of California, Los Angeles. Surprisingly, the initial message that was sent through the internet was "LO." In fact, scientists planned to send work "Log in"; however, only the initial two letters were able to reach their destination at second network node build at Stanford Research Institute and prior to the transmission of the next three letters, the network was down because of a glitch. Quickly the error was fixed, and scientists resent the message.

The main task that ARPANET had to carry out was to develop the rules for communication known as protocols for communicating through ARPANET. Therefore, ARPANET specifically played a significant role in the development of protocols required for internetworking, in which various separate networks could be linked through a network of networks. This led to the development of the TCP/IP protocol suite, which postulates the major guidelines for joining and communicating through ARPANET.

After the development of ARPANET, in 1986, NSF (National Science Foundation) backbone was developed, and computing centers of 5 universities of the United States US were connected to form NSFnet. The Universities which participated are mentioned below:

i.   Princeton University - John von Neumann National Supercomputer Center, JvNC

ii. The University of Illinois at Urbana-Champaign - National Center for Supercomputing Applications, NCSA

iii. Cornell University - Cornell Theory Center, CTC

iv. General Atomics - San Diego Supercomputer Center, SDSC

v.   Carnegie Mellon University - Pittsburgh Supercomputer Center, PSC

NFSnet was the successor of ARPAnet and became widely popular by 1990, after which ARPANET was decommissioned. Several other universities and countries developed different networks in parallel (Claffy, Braun and Polyzos 1994). In 1965, National Physical Laboratory (NPL) suggested a packing switching network. In 1966, Michigan Educational Research Information Triad developed the MERIT network by using funds and support from the State of Michigan and the National Science Foundation (NSF). In 1973, a packet switching network, identified as CYCLADES, was developed by France. Thus, several parallel systems were operating on different protocols, which led scientists to start looking for some common standard to interconnect the networks. TCP/IP protocol suits were developed by 1978, and by 1983, they were implemented by ARPANET.

The integration of two big networks came about in 1981. NFS developed the Computer Science Network (CSNET), and it was connected to ARPANET through TCP/IP protocol suite. This network was not just popular in the research community but also greatly admired by the private sector. Originally NFS supported speed of only 56 kbit/s, which was later upgraded to in 1988 to 1.5 Mbit/s to ease the growth of network through involving merit network, MCA, IBM, and the state of Michigan.

Several corporate entities participated in the development of this network once they realized its merits and strength. Consequently, by the late 1980s, numerous Internet Service Providers (ISPs) began providing support for carrying the network traffic. Subsequently, NFSNET was expanded and later upgraded to provide speed up to 45Mbit/s by 1991. Various commercial ISPs played their part by providing backbone serve and were popular amid the corporate. However, in 1995, NFSNET was decommissioned to facilitate the commercial usage of the network, and presently the Internet carries commercial traffic.

Presently, throughout the world, several hundred universities and research centers are connected to it. Due to the popularity of this network in the research community, the National Research and Education Network (NREN) was created in 1991 and the World Wide Web was released. In the beginning, the role of the internet was just to transfer files. The acclaim of the internet we see today goes to Tim Berners-Lee, who introduced the World Wide Web. With the arrival of the World Wide Web, the use of the network was transformed. Now, we can use this web of information to recover any information accessible over the internet. In 1992, Software called the browser was created by researchers at the University of Illinois to browse the internet. This browser, known as Mosaic, has enabled us to browse the internet in a manner we browse it at present.

Internet Addresses

There are millions of devices connected to the internet which necessitates some mechanism that can be used to identify every device connected to the internet distinctively. Moreover, we also need some centralized approach to take care of this mechanism so that the symbols used for identifying each device connected to the internet do not get duplicate; otherwise, the whole purpose will be crushed. To take care of this, experts have developed a centralized authority identified as Internet Assigned Numbers Authority (IANA). This authority is responsible for to assign a unique 32-bit binary number, which is known as IP (Internet Protocol) address. An IP address is divided into four octets with each of the octets having eight binary digits. A dot is used to separate these octets. Below mentioned is an example of such an IP address

11011011.00001000.10111100.10101110

An octet contains 8-bits and can only have two binary values that are 1 and 0. Hence, the minimum value each octet can have is 0., i.e. 00000000; whereas, the maximum value an octet can have is 256, i.e. 11111111 ($2^8 = 256$).

It is difficult to remember this 32-bit address in binary, therefore, for our better and easier understanding, it is expressed in a decimal format. Nevertheless, this decimal format is only for human understanding. The computer only understands it in the binary presentation, whereas the above IP address is expressed in decimal as 219.8.188.174. These octets are employed to form and different discrete classes. There are two parts of an IP address, namely, **Network** and **Host. The** Network part in IP is used for identifying the network to which it belongs; whereas, the host part is used for identifying the device of a specific network.

The IP address of a device uniquely identifies different devices connected to the internet. Its function can be thought of as similar to the postal system where we identify any specific house by firstly identifying the country, then province/state, district, post office, block, and finally, the house number. IP addresses have been classified into five categories based on the availability of IP range. These categories are as under:

Table Error! No text of specified style in document.**-1 IP Address categories**

Class / category	Address range	Supports
Class A	1.0.0.1 to 126.255.255.254	Provides support to 16 million hosts on each of 127 networks.
Class B	128.1.0.1 to 191.255.255.254	Provides support to 65,000 hosts on each of 16,000 networks.
Class C	192.0.1.1 to 223.255.254.254	Provides support to 254 hosts on each of 2 million networks
Class D	224.0.0.0 to 239.255.255.255	This class is reserved for multicast groups
Class E	240.0.0.0 to 254.255.255.254	This class is reserved for future use, or Research and

		Development purposes.

Internet Assigned Numbers Authority (IANA) has the responsibility of assigning the IP addresses through the allocation of the large chunk of IP addresses to 5 Regional Internet Registries (RIRs). These registries are, in turn, responsible for allocating the IP addresses in their respective zones. Below mentioned is the list of these RIRs along with their area of operations:

i. ARIN- This RIR is responsible for serving North America and several regions of the North Atlantic and Caribbean islands.

ii. APNIC- This RIR is responsible for serving the Asia Pacific zone.

iii. LACNIC- This RIR is responsible for serving Latin America and the Caribbean regions

iv. AfriNIC- This RIR is responsible for serving the African zone.

v. RIPE NCC- This RIR is responsible for serving Europe, parts of Central Asia, and the Middle East.

An organization, namely, Number Resource Organization (NRO) is responsible for liaison and coordinating among the above five RIRs

DNS

While browsing any website on the internet, we type something similar to www.uou.ac.in that is, we do not deal with IP addresses such as 104.28.2.92. However, the truth is that even if we type http:\\ 106.25.2.82 in the URL, we will be landed on the same webpage. We are quite accustomed to and comfortable in using and memorizing the names of the websites instead of a number. Besides, with time, these IP address changes and few of the sites contain more than one IP address. Furthermore, we can only transfer data over the internet by using IP addresses since the routing of the packet of data that is sent through the internet, is carried out using the IP address. There is a server known as Domain Name System (DNS). This server is responsible for taking care of this translation job to make this process simple and to save us from the trouble of memorizing these changing IP address numbers. Every time we type an address such as http:\\www.uou.ac.in, a background procedure known as DNS name resolution is initiated. Our computers keep the footpath of lately visited websites and locally preserves a database in the cache of DNS. If the IP address of the website we have requested is not found in the DNS cache of our local computer, then the subsequent possible place to find it is in the DNS server of our Internet Service Provider (ISP). These DNS servers of our Internet Service Provider also maintain the cache of the lately visited webpages. In case the information is not available even in the DNS server of ISP, it then forwards the query to the root name servers, which publish the root zone file to both other DNS servers as well as clients on the Internet. The root zone file designates the location of the authoritative servers for the DNS top-level domains (abbreviated as TLD). Presently, there are 13 root name servers which are listed below:

1. VeriSign Global Registry Services

2. University of Southern California - Information Sciences Institute

3. Cogent Communications

4. University of Maryland

5. NASA Ames Research Center

6. Internet Systems Consortium, Inc.

7. U.S. DOD Network Information Center

8. U.S. Army Research Lab

9. Autonomica/NORDUnet

10. VeriSign Global Registry Services

11. RIPE NCC (Réseaux IP Européens Network Coordination Centre)

12. ICANN (Internet Corporation for Assigned Names and Numbers)

13. WIDE Project

These root name servers guide the request to the suitable Top-Level Domain name servers by way of first reading the latter part of the URL. We have quoted the example of http:\\www.uou.ac.in. The last part of this URL is .in. Few other examples of TLD name servers include .org, .com, .biz, .in, .us, etc. These Top-Level Domain name servers play the role of a switchboard and guide our request to the suitable authoritative name server retained by each domain. Such an authoritative name server also maintains other beneficial information along with maintaining DNS records. The record of address is reverted back to the host computer requesting it through TLD name servers, ISP's DNS server, and name servers.

Such an intermediate server maintains the record of this IP address in the cache of their DNS so that they don't have to go through the trouble of this process once again in case if they receive the same request. In case if the same URL is demanded over again, the DNS cache of that localhost PC will return the IP address of the requested URL.

Internet Infrastructure

As apparent by its name, Internet, is a collection of various small, medium as well as large networks. This undoubtedly points out one fact, which is that no single body is the owner of the internet, thereby making it a major proven example of collaborative success. It is indeed amazing that how such a huge network extended across the continents is running successfully without any problem. Naturally, we indeed need an international body for monitoring such a huge network, which can set the rules, guidelines, and protocols to join and expand this network. Hence, in 1992, an international organization, famous as "The Internet Society," was created to take care of the above-stated concerns.

Let's take a brief look at the working of the internet. Consider a scenario. We send an email to our friend who receives it on his/her computer located in another country or even another continent. While we are working on our computer without connecting it to the internet, our computer at that instant is a standalone system (Stoica et al. 2002). However, when we connect our computer to the internet using a modem, we become a part of the network. The Internet Service Provider (ISP) is the link amid the internet backbone, by the help of which the routing of data to the user takes place. The ISP is responsible for connecting us to the internet backbone at Network

Access Points (NAP). Various large telecommunication companies provide these Network Access Points in several regions (DiGiorgio and Bender 2002). Such large telecommunication companies are in charge of connecting the countries and the continents through building as well as maintaining the huge support/ backbone infrastructure to route data from one NAP to another NAP. ISPs are linked to this backbone infrastructure at NAP and have the responsibility of building and managing networks locally. Therefore, when we connect our computer to the internet by dialing through modem, we primarily become part of the local ISP, which further connects us to the internet backbone via NAP. Through this backbone, our requested data is routed and delivered to the desired destination NAP, where the ISP of our friend's network is sited. The moment when our friend connects his computer to the internet by dialing through the modem, that data is delivered to his computer.

World Wide Web

We often interchangeably use the terms World Wide Web and internet, or sometimes we simply use the word 'web.' In reality, the web is just one of the numerous services provided by the internet. Few popular services other than the web provided by the internet include Usenet, e-mail, FTP, messaging service, etc. To establish communication over the internet and exchanging information, the web makes use of HTTP protocol. The web was developed in 1989 at CERN (European de Researchers Nucleaires), by an English scientist named Tim Berners-Lee. The web is composed of all the public web sites as well as all the devices which access the content of the web. As a matter of fact, WWW is an information-sharing model and has been developed for exchanging information over the internet. Innumerable public websites consisting of a collection of web pages, are accessible through the internet. These websites hold abundant information in the form of audios, videos, texts, and picture format. We access these web pages through an application software known as a web browser. A few examples of the well-known web browser include Chrome, Firefox, Safari, Internet Explorer, etc. After having an overview of the cyber world, now, we will discuss the protection of cyber (internet) connected systems from cyber-attacks, its importance.

Aspects of Cybersecurity

As the cyber world (internet) is extremely vulnerable to attacks by cybercriminals and hackers, it is essential to equip our systems with cybersecurity protocols. So while discussing cybersecurity, one might think that who are we trying to protect ourselves from?" The answer is that there are three significant aspects we are trying to control, which include:

- Unauthorized Access

- Unauthorized Modification

- Unauthorized Deletion

The terms mentioned above are synonymous with the very popular CIA triad, which is a model developed to guide policies for the security of information in any organization. CIA stands for Confidentiality, Integrity, and Availability. We also commonly refer to the CIA triad as three pillars of security, and the majority of the security policies of any organization are founded on these three principles.

The CIA Triad

The CIA triad is a model designed to guide the formation of security policies in organizations and companies. It is sometimes also referred to as the AIC triad to avoid mix-up with the Central Intelligence Agency (CIA). The three components of the CIA triad are thought of as the most fundamental and significant components of security. Let's have a look at these three components.

The model of CIA triad consisting of Confidentiality, Integrity, and Availability has been designed and developed to provide guidelines to the organization for the formation of Cyber Security policies in the territory of Information security

Confidentiality

Confidentiality defines the rules which restrict the access of data/information. Confidentiality takes on the precautionary actions to limit sensitive data from being accessed by hackers or cyber attackers.

In any organization, employees are permitted or denied the access of data as per its type and sensitivity by only granting the right persons access to that data in a department. Quite often, they are also properly trained about the sharing of data and securing their accounts by using only strong passwords.

In any organization, the way of handling information can be changed to ensure its protection. There are different ways to ensure confidentiality, such as Data encryption, two-factor authentication, biometric verification, data classification, and security tokens.

Integrity

Integrity guarantees that the data is correct, consistent, and trustworthy over the period, which means that data must not be illegally accessed, altered, or deleted within any transit.

In any organization, proper actions need to be taken to ensure the safety of data. Ways of controlling the breach of information include making use of file permissions and user access control methods. Moreover, different tools and technologies should be developed and implemented to detect any illegal alteration or a breach in the data. Several organizations verify the integrity of their data by using a checksum, or even cryptographic checksum.

Additionally, there must be regular back-ups to cope with the unexpected loss of data or any accidental deletion of data or even cyber-attacks. Presently, the most trusted and popular solution for this is cloud backups.

Availability

The last component of the CIA triad is Availability. All essential constituents, like software, hardware, devices, security equipment, and networks, should be upheld and upgraded. This measure will result in uninterrupted operations with convenient data access. The provision of constant communication among various components must be ensured by providing sufficient bandwidth.

In case of bottlenecks or disaster situations, availability also includes the arrangement of surplus security equipment. Utilities such as firewalls, proxy servers, an appropriate backup solution, and disaster recovery plans must ensure the handling of DoS attacks.

A successful methodology involves multiple security layers to guarantee the protection of every component of Cybersecurity. For instance, the protection of computers, networks, software programs, the data, and hardware systems is essential for a successful protection methodology.

Need for Cybersecurity

It is an established fact that people in today's world spend most of their time on the internet. Most of the internet users are practically unaware of the mechanisms of the online data transfers, and this is a golden situation for the hackers. With numerous access points, constant traffic, public IP's, and availability of enormous data to exploit, it is quite convenient for the black hat hackers to exploit the vulnerabilities by making malicious software. Presently, cyber-attacks are growing rapidly with every passing day. Hackers have become cleverer and more innovative with their cyber-attacks and how they dodge firewalls and virus scans still amazes a lot of people.

Considering all the threats and vulnerabilities, all internet users need to possess countermeasure systems to protect them against the plethora of cyber-attacks. In this way, we will be able to protect our data from falling into the wrong hands. Therefore, cybersecurity is essential to safeguard our systems in the vulnerable world of the internet.

Chapter Two

Introduction to Cyber-crimes

Introduction

Cyber-crime is a type of crime involving the usage of digital technologies in the commission of a felony, directed to communication and computing technologies. The contemporary techniques are thriving the use of internet activities, which has resulted in generating exploitation and has significantly increased susceptibility making an appropriate manner of transferring intimate data to commit a felony through illegitimate activity. Illegal activities involve various offenses such as online transaction theft or fraud, an attack on Information center Data System, internet sale fraud, child pornography built images and also partaking in positioning malicious internet activities like email scams, viruses, third party abuse such as phishing, and worm etc. As per the worldwide approach, the internet must be kept safe from any illegal or unlawful activity by enforcement of different levels of firewall settings to monitor and avoid crimes taking place in cyberspace. To avoid the entree of hackers in networks, different network security controls are employed which includes virtual private networks (VPNs), firewalls, and various encryption algorithms. Out of these three, the virtual private network (VPNs) plays a significant part in inhibiting hackers from gaining access to the networks. These networks deliver such a method to end users so that they may access information privately on their network through a public network infrastructure like the internet.

The earliest cyber-crime which was recorded took place in 1820, which is hardly surprising keeping in mind the fact that the abacus, which is considered to be the most primitive form of the computer, was invented around 3500 B.C. in Japan, India, and China. However, the epoch of the latest computers instigated with the advent of the analytical engine of Charles Babbage.

A textile manufacturer, named, Joseph-Marie Jacquard, produced the loom in France in the year 1820. This particular device permitted the recurrence of a series of footsteps in the weaving of distinctive fabrics. This led to generating a fear amid workers of Jacquard that their conventional employment and income were being threatened. Consequently, his employees' started committing acts of sabotage to dispirit Jacquard from further using the latest technology. This was the first-ever noted cyber-crime.

Computers of today's age have come a long way, with the advent of neural networks and nano-computing devices capable of turning every atom in a glass of water into a computer having the ability to perform millions of operations every second.

One reason for the rise in cyber-crimes today is the increasing dependence of humans on computers in this modern era. In a time when everything from cooking stoves and fridges to huge nuclear power plants is being controlled through computers, cyber-crimes have assumed somewhat threatening implications. In the past years, some of the significant cyber-crimes which took place include the Citibank rip off during which 10 million US $ were deceitfully transferred from a bank into another bank account in Switzerland.

This attack was executed by a Russian hacker group headed by Vladimir Kevin, who was a renowned hacker of his time. The group of hackers compromised the security systems of the bank. Apparently, Vladimir Kevin was making use of his office computer at AO Saturn, a computer firm situated in St. Petersburg, Russia, to get into the computers of Citibank. He was eventually arrested from Heathrow airport while traveling to Switzerland.

Defining Cyber-Crime

Let us first define "cyber-crime" and understand how it is different from a "conventional Crime." Computer crimes can include conventional criminal offenses, like forgery, theft, scam, defamation, and malice. All of these crimes are subject to the Penal Codes. Such type of computer abuses have also given rise to several modern crimes which are addressed by the Information Technology Act, 2000.

It is not appropriate to define cyber-crimes, as "actions which carry a punishment by the Information Technology Act" since the Indian Penal Code also covers several cyber-crimes, for example, cyber defamation, email spoofing, and sending intimidating emails, etc. We can simply define cyber-crime as unlawful actions in which the computer is either a target or a tool or else both".

Let have a look at the acts where the computer is used as a tool for an illegal act. This type of activity generally consists of a variation of a traditional crime by using computers. Few examples are given in the following text:

Email Spoofing

An email is known as spoofed email is it seems to originate from one source where in reality, it has been sent from another source. For example, the email address of Sunita is sunita@indianlaws.org. Her enemy, Raveena, spoofs her e-mail ID and sends offensive texts to all her connections. As the e-mails seem to have come from Sunita, her friends might take offense, and her friendships could be ruined for life.

One implication of email spoofing can be loss of money. In one case, an American youngster made billions of dollars by disseminating incorrect information about a few particular companies whose shares he had short traded. He spread this incorrect information by sending spoofed emails, allegedly from news agencies such as Reuters to investors and share brokers who were told that the companies were performing poorly. The share values did not go back to their initial levels even after the truth came out hence causing loss of millions of dollars to the thousands of investors.

Forgery

Fake currency notes, revenue stamps, and postage, mark sheets, etc. can be forged with the help of sophisticated computers, scanners, and printers scanners (Snail 2009). One even finds vendors lobbying the sale of forged certificates and even mark sheets outside numerous colleges in Asia. Such mark sheets or certificates are produced using computers, and high-quality printers and scanners. As a matter of fact, this has grown into a thriving business involving hundreds of Rupees being taken from the student in exchange for these fake but authentic-looking degrees and certificates.

Cyber Defamation

Cyber defamation takes place when defamation occurs using the internet or computers. For example, somebody broadcasts defamatory stuff about particular someone on a website or else broadcasts e-mails comprising defamatory information to all contacts of that person.

One recent example is when a young girl, namely, Surekha (real names of people have not been used), was about to be married to Suraj. The girl was really happy because even though it was an arranged marriage, she had developed liking for the boy. The boy seemed nice and open-minded. Later, one day when Surekha met Suraj, he looked anxious and quite upset. He did not appear to have any interest in talking to her. Upon asking, he told her that his family members had been receiving e-mails containing mean things about Surekha's character. A few emails mentioned her past. He further informed her that his parents were just very upset and were thinking of breaking off their engagement. Luckily, Suraj succeeded in agreeing with his parents and the other elders of his family to contact the police instead of believing in those mails without verification.

In the course of investigation, it was exposed that the person responsible for sending those e-mails was none other than the stepfather of Surekha. Her stepfather had sent those e-mails with the intention to break up the marriage. In the case of Surekha's marriage, he was to lose control of her property, of which he was the legal custodian till her marriage.

One more popular case of cyber defamation took place in America. All friends and family of a woman were harassed with offensive email messages which appeared to be received from her email account. These offensive emails were damaging the repute of the woman among her family and friends. That woman was a popular activist against pornography. In actuality, a group of people who did not agree with her point of view and were angry with her for differing with them had decided to malign her repute by using such sly techniques. Besides sending spoofed offensive e-mails, those people also put up websites about her, which essentially defamed her character.

Cyberstalking

In the Oxford dictionary, cyberstalking is defined as "pursuing stealthily". Cyberstalking includes following the actions of a person across the Internet through posting messages (occasionally intimidating) on the notice boards visited by the victim, continually bombarding the victim with emails and entering into the chat-rooms which are frequently visited by the victim, etc.

Information on Cyber-Crime

In the start of a particular development period, people were quietly driven to accomplish decent progress in prevailing technological activities. From the time of the start of the civilization period, humans have always been inspired by their necessities to make better progress in the prevailing technologies. In 1969, the design of a super parallel network called ARPANET (Advanced Research Project Agency) was made. ARPANET was composed of more than fifty computers connected with web links to facilitate military operations. These networks gradually grew and later became popular by the name of online Internet activity to share business systems where communication was carried out in Cyberspace.

The term Cyberlaw denotes the legal jurisdiction and other means of previous regulatory aspects on the internet. This process is a constantly generic one. At the time when an internet development strategy is made, various modifications are enforced during its development, as a result of which various legal concerns also gets developed via illicit activists. Child Pornography is one of the severe cybercrime on the Internet. Online pedophiles devise ways to engage kids in sexual activities using the Internet. Likewise, the traffic threats, distribution of indecent material, and posting of pornography with all its dirty exposure are some of the most significant known criminal cyber offenses nowadays. Such offenses, in reality, impends to defy the development of technology and also leave a perpetual scar and destruction on the younger generation, if not restricted.

In the world of cybercrime, a rather distinctive form of harassment is Cyber annoyance. Several types of harassment occur in cyberspace or by using cyberspace to reach criminal offenses. Different forms of harassment can be racial, sexual, religious, or any other. People involved in executing these types of harassment are guilty of cybercrimes. Harassments and Stalking are among issues that numerous people, particularly women, face in their real-life.

One more type of cybercrime is cybercrime against property in varied forms. Such criminal offenses consist of unsanctioned computer trespass via cyberspaces, destruction of computer, and transmission of harmful programs and unauthorized tenure of computerized information. Until presently, cracking and hacking are among the largest known cybercrimes. Hacking is known as breaking into a computer system without the will and knowing of the authorized person, interfering with the valuable and private information or data. Utilizing one's programming capabilities as well as hiring different programmers to attain access to a network or a specific computer via unauthorized access are among serious criminal offenses. Similarly, the making and distribution of damaging computer programs or any type of nasty viruses or software which causes permanent damage to network or computer systems are another types of cybercrime, and such type of software piracy is also another discrete form of cybercrime. Numerous people in the cyber world disseminate illegal and unofficial pirated copies of software products for monetary benefits.

One more form of cybercrime is a crime against administration. In this type of cybercrime, the most distinct kind is Cyber Terrorism. With the increase in the use of the internet, several individuals or groups have arisen, which uses cyberspace to threaten the worldwide governments and to terrify the residents of the country. This crime exhibits when a group or an individual "cracks" or hacks into a military or government maintained website. We can classify cyber-crimes into three broad categories which are:

1) Crime against the Individuals

It can be further categorized into crimes against:

- Person
- Property of an individual.

2) Crime against Organization

It can be further categorized into crimes against:

- Government
- Any Firm, Company, or Group of Individuals.

3) Crime against Society

Below mentioned are examples of some specific crimes which are committed against the above mentioned different groups

Crimes against Individuals

      a.   Cyber-stalking.

      b.   Harassment through electronic mails

      c.   Email spoofing.

      d.   Defamation.

      e.   Indecent or Offensive exposure.

      f.   Broadcasting indecent material.

      g.   Unauthorized control/access over network or computer system.

      h.   Cheating.

      i.   Fraud.

Crimes Against Individual Property

      a.   Unauthorized access/control over network or computer system

      b.   Computer vandalism

      c.   Net repass.

      d.   Spreading virus.

e.   Crimes against intellectual property

f.   Internet thefts

Crimes Against Organization

a.   Cyber terrorism against any military or government organization.

b.   Possession of or control over unauthorized data or information.

c.   Unauthorized access/control over network or computer system.

d.   Dissemination of Pirate software.

Crimes Against Society

a.   Trafficking.

b.   Child pornography

c.   Indecent exposure to youth.

d.   Forgery.

e.   Online gambling.

f.   Sale of banned articles.

The Department of Justice for cybercrime has classified the utilization of computer in cyber-crime into following three ways:

- Crimes where a computer is used as a weapon – making use of a computer as a tool to commit "orthodox crime" in the physical world (for example, committing fraud or engaging in illegal gambling).

- Crimes where a computer is used as a target - attacking the other computers or networks (An example is spreading of viruses).

- Crimes where a computer is essentially used as an accessory – making use of a computer for storing any type of illegal information.

How Cyber Criminals Work

Cyber-crimes have gained the status of profession presently, and the demography of the cyber-criminal is altering promptly with the type of organized criminals who are more conventionally linked with crimes such as extortion, drug-trafficking, and money laundering. Cyber-criminals can obtain details of bank accounts data or credit cards by using different illegal methods, each involving its own comparative combinations of skills, risk, and expense. The possible marketplace for such type of transaction is a secreted Internet Relay Chat (IRC) chat room. Another method increasingly used by criminals to gain control of a bank account is through phishing. Different phishing tools are available in the market at cheap rates.

The cybercriminals mostly operate in the following manners:

Coders

Coders are the qualified experts among the hacking community. After gaining experience of few years in this art and establishing number of contacts, they produce ready-to-use tools (such as mailers, Trojans, custom bots) or provide different services (for example making such a binary code which can't be detected by AV engines) to the cyber-crime labor force – the 'kids.' Coders generally earn a few hundred dollars for every illegal activity they are involved in.

Kids

The name of this group is because of their tender age; most are under 18. Kids engage in buying, trading, and reselling of the fundamental building blocks of effective cyber-scams like PHP mailers, spam lists, credit card numbers, proxies, hacked hosts, and scam pages etc. Generally, kids earn far less, mostly due to the frequency of being 'ripped off' by each other.

Drops

The criminals who come in this category convert the 'virtual money' acquired through cyber-crimes into real cash. They are generally located in countries where laws of e-crimes are rather sloppy (such as Malaysia, Bolivia, and Indonesia). Such countries represent 'safe' addresses for buying of goods through stolen financial details, or else 'safe' authentic bank accounts where money can be illegally transferred, or paid unlawfully.

Mobs

Mobs are professionally functioning criminal organizations that engage in all of the functions mentioned above. Systematized crime generally makes good use of safe 'drops.' Mobs mostly recruit skillful 'coders' onto their payrolls.

Types of Cyber Hackers

White Hat Hackers

This type of hacker includes ethical hackers who ethically are against the abuse of computer systems. A white-hat hacker mostly concentrates on safeguarding IT systems, while the aim of a black hat hacker (the opposite of white hat hacker) is to break into such IT or computer systems. Often we use the term 'white hat hacker' to refer to those hackers who attempt to break into networks or systems to help the possessors of the system by informing them about security flaws or to carry out any other noble activity. Various computer security companies employ such white hat hackers; these professionals are also sometimes known as sneakers. Groups of such hackers are often referred to as tiger teams.

Black Hat Hackers

A black hat hacker is an individual who compromises a computer system's security without the consent of an authorized party, usually with wicked intentions. Likewise, activity is software cracking in which copy prevention devices in the software are overcome, which might or might not be lawful in a country. The main difference between a black and a white-hat hacker is that a white hat hacker claims to follow ethical values. Just like black hat hackers, often white hat hackers are closely aware of the internal details of security systems of any company and can dig into vague machine code when they are required to find a way out to any complex encountered problem. Few use the word grey hat and even fewer use the term 'brown hat' to define activities of someone crossing between white and black.

Gray Hat Hackers

In the computer security community, a Gray Hat is used to refer to a skilled hacker who occasionally acts lawfully, at times in goodwill, and at times not. Gray Hat hackers are a hybrid among black and white hat hackers. Generally, they do not hack for their personal benefit or for wicked intentions. However, they may or may not intermittently commit offenses throughout their technological exploits.

Internet Crime Hackers

These hackers commit different crimes on the internet, using the Internet. The term 'Internet crime' is rather a generic term which includes various crimes such as credit card frauds, phishing, illegal downloading, scams, industrial espionage, bank robbery, child pornography, kidnapping of kids through chat rooms, creation and dissemination of viruses, cyber terrorism, Spam and so on. All such crimes are facilitated through computers. Various types of Internet crime differ in their design and ease of availability to be committed.

Blackmail Hackers

Blackmail is an extensively established unlawful act which has been given a novel twist in the present age. The person who blackmails may threaten to issue humiliating or other detrimental information through the Internet in case the victim does not agree to comply with the demands of the criminal. This type of cybercrime might reach as far as the victim being forced to transfer money to an untraceable bank account by making use of some type of online payment program, thereby using modern technology for committing the crime. Blackmail hackers generally hack official or military websites, work on cyber-crime operations for making money, or hack online credit card.

General Tips to Get Protected from Cyber-crime

Following are a few general tips to protect computer systems from the growing threats.

End Online Session Completely

Just closing the window of the browser or entering the address of a new website without properly logging out might provide hackers a chance to gain access to information on our account. Therefore, it is advisable to always terminate our online session properly by clicking on the "Sign Out or Log out" button. Additionally, one should avoid availing the option of "remember" your username and password data.

Create Backup of Significant Data

It is advisable to create a backup of all the significant files, whether professional or personal. Getting accustomed to back up our files repeatedly is considered the foremost step towards the security of our personal computers.

Using Security Programs

It is advisable to buy an internet security program for our computer in case our computer system does not have data protection software for online protection. Nowadays, the majority of all new computer systems in the market come with some type of already installed security programs.

Protect Your Password

A password should consist of a combination of numbers, letters (both lower case and upper case), and special characters. Moreover, passwords should be regularly altered and must not be shared with other people.

Participation in Social Networking

Personal information must not be exposed to others while engaging in social networking sites. All such sites normally have a certain degree of control over security concerns. Privacy settings should be used to avoid spreading of personal information.

Using One's Own Computer

It's normally safer to access financial accounts only from one's own computer system. In case of using any other computer, always remember to clear all "History" as well as delete all the "Temporary Internet Files" after logging out of your account.

Regular Updating of Software Package

Regular and timely online updates are required for the proper functioning of all the Internet security software installed on one's computer system.

Using Email

One general rule is to not click on any links received in emails from people we do not know. Hackers often make to use of E-mail as their major target to steal personal information, security codes, financial data, and other important information. So the use of such links should be avoided. If we require access to any website, we can visit that website by manually typing the address in our menu bar. Various countries across the world have started to implement laws and other related regulatory mechanisms to reduce the frequency of cybercrimes. In many countries, the rules on the effectiveness of the inhibition and punishment of computer crime need a vigorous number and even the proceedings which lag far behind the actuality of demand for cyber-crimes in judicial practice.

Chapter Three

Classification of Cyber Attacks

Introduction

The information held by the computer system of any organization can be compromised in several ways, such as through unintentional or malicious actions, or simply as a result of software failure or the failure of electronic components. Even though we must take into account all of these potential hazards, malicious internet attacks are damaging the organizations in a serious manner. In 2014, a survey on Information Security Breaches was conducted, which indicated that 81% of big companies had reported incidents of some type of security breach, costing those organizations an average amid £600,000 and £1.5m. Such findings are also backed by routine incidents of large scale cyber incidents, for example, the Gameover ZeuS botnet incident.

A cyber-attack is a deliberate manipulation of networks, computer systems, as well as technology-dependent enterprises. Cyber-attacks employ harmful code for modification of computer data, code, or logic, which leads to harmful consequences compromising our data and disseminate cyber-crimes like theft of identity and information. We also recognize a cyber-attack as a computer network attack (CNA).

Although the term 'cyber-attack' is a generic terminology comprising a large number of topics, nonetheless few of the well-known are:

i. Misuse of resources

ii. Illegal access to the targeted system and gaining access to sensitive data

iii. Altering data and systems stored within

iv. Making use of ransomware attacks for encryption of data and extraction of money from victims

v. Disturbing normal functioning of the business and its related processes

Presently, cyberattacks are becoming more advanced and refined, making it a complicated task for every business and security analyst to deal with this challenge and protect computer systems against these attacks.

In today's world, where online transactions increasingly drive our everyday tasks, big data, information managed, or saved through the internet, social networks, and automated procedures carried out via the use of different IT systems, data privacy, and information security are constantly facing risks. Cyber-crimes are constantly increasing with the development of advanced techniques and tools. New tools are being developed to gain unauthorized access to data, networks, and programs which compromise the integrity, confidentiality, and accessibility of information. With every passing year, the number of attacks is not only increasing but such attacks by defeating the security of big companies, are badly affecting the security of data, business continuity as well as the trust of customers (Pan Morris and Adhikari 2015). Due to the increasing number of attacks, 2014 was internationally recognized as "the year of cyber-attacks."

Types of Cyber Threats

To understand the requirement for Cybersecurity measures and their practices, we will first have a brief look at different types of cyber-attacks and threats.

Phishing Attacks

Phishing is normally used for stealing user data like login credentials and credit card numbers. Phishing takes place when an invader, posturing as a trusted individual, deceits the victim into opening an email, text message, or instant message. The prey is then tricked into opening a malicious link which can freeze the system as part of a ransomware attack, disclosing sensitive data, or installation of malware.

Such breach of data can leave a disastrous impact. For an individual, it includes stealing funds, identity theft, or unsanctioned purchases. Quite often, phishing is used for gaining a foothold in corporate or government networks as part of a more substantial plot, for instance, an advanced persistent threat (APT). In such incidents, workers are compromised to attain access to secured information of the company and to bypass security parameters.

Spear Phishing Attacks

This type of attack is an email aimed at a specific organization or individual, wanting unauthorized access to critical information.

Spear phishing hacks are not performed by any random attackers but are most likely carried out by individuals out for financial advantage, trade secrets, or military intelligence.

Such emails seem to be received from an individual working inside the receiver's organization or from someone personally known by the receiver. Most of the time, such activities are performed by government-sponsored hackers. Cybercriminals also perform such attacks to resell confidential information to private companies as well as to governments. Such attackers make use of social engineering and individually-built tactics to successfully personalize messages and websites.

Whale Phishing Attack

This is a type of phishing which focuses on high-profile employees, for instance, the CEO or CFO of the company. The purpose of this attack is to steal crucial data since employees holding higher positions in an organization have unrestricted access to sensitive data. The majority of whaling cases manipulate the target into authorizing high-value wire transfers to the assailant.

This term 'whaling' denotes the size of the attack. Whales are targeted subject to their position in an organization. As they are greatly targeted, such attacks are harder to notice comparative to the standard phishing attacks. In any business, such hacks can be reduced by system security administrators by encouraging the corporate staff to participate in training on security awareness.

Malware Attacks

Malware attacks are a type of code made to silently disturb a compromised computer system without the approval of the user. This expansive definition comprises several certain types of malevolent software like ransomware, command, spyware, and control.

Various popular states, businesses, and criminal actors have been caught up deploying malware. Malware is not like other software in a sense that it can be distributed across a network, bring alterations and harm without getting detected. Moreover, it can be persistently present in the infected system; thereby can potentially destroy a network and bring the performance of a machine to its knees.

Ransomware

Ransomware blocks access to the data of the target data, generally threatening to erase the data in case ransom is not paid. However, even paying the ransom does not guarantee regaining access to the data. This activity is mostly carried out through a Trojan transporting a payload masked as a legitimate file.

Drive-by Attack

This is a common way of disseminating malware. A cyber attacker searches for any website which is not secured and plants a malign script into HTTP or PHP in one of the website pages. That script can install malware into the computer system visiting that website or else become an IFRAME redirecting the browser of the target to a particular site controlled by the attacker. In majority cases, such scripts are obscured, making the code complex for analyzing by security researchers. The term drive-by is used for these attacks since they don't need any action on the target's part except paying a visit to the compromised website. After visiting the compromised site, victims robotically and silently get infected if their computer system is susceptible to malware, particularly if they don't have updated security measures.

Trojan Horses

A Trojan is a type of malicious software program which falsely presents itself to look useful. They look like routine software and spread by urging a target to install them by appearing beneficial. Among all the types of malware, Trojans are thought as the most dangerous, since they often target to steal financial information.

Web Attacks

SQL Injection

SQL injection is also called as SQLI. SQL is a particular type of attack which uses malicious code for manipulating backend databases to attain data that was not wished-for display. Such data may consist of various items such as private customer details, private data of company, and user lists.

SQLI can cause destructing effects on a business. An effective SQLI attack can result in the deletion of complete tables, unsanctioned inspecting of user lists, and in few cases, the attacker can attain administrative access to a database, making it extremely destructive for a business. While calculating the expected price of SQLI, we must take into consideration the loss of customer faith in case personal information of the customer, such as details of credit card details, addresses, and phone numbers are stolen. Even though SQLI can be employed to attack any SQL database, the criminals frequently target websites.

Cross-Site Scripting

Cross-site scripting (abbreviated as XSS) is a type of injection breach where the criminal transmits malign code into content from otherwise trustworthy websites. Such incidents take place when an uncertain source is permitted to attach its own (malign) code into different web applications, making the malign code bundled together with other content, which is then directed to the browser of the victim.

Attackers normally send malign code in the form of fragments of the Javascript code implemented by the browser of the victim. The exploits consist of malign executable scripts in various languages such as HTML, Java, Flash, and Ajax. Cross-site scripting attacks can be extremely destructive; nonetheless, dealing with susceptibilities enabling such attacks is comparatively simple.

Distributed Denial-of-Service (DDoS) Attack

The aim of Denial-of-service (DDoS) is to shut down a service or network, making it unreachable to its intended users. The attackers attain their aim through crushing the victim with the traffic load or else flooding it with data, which activates a crash. In both circumstances, the DoS attack denies genuine users like account holders, and company employees.

The targets of DDoS attacks are often web servers of prestigious organizations like government and trade organizations, commerce, media companies, and banking. Even though such attacks don't lead to theft or loss of crucial data or other assets, still such attacks can cost the target loads of time and money to mitigate. DDoS is frequently employed in combination to divert from attacks of another network

Password Attack

A password attack is an effort to obtain or else decrypt the password of the user with maligned intentions. Different techniques are used by crackers such as dictionary attacks, password sniffers, and cracking programs in password attacks. Even though there are some defense mechanisms against such attacks, however normally, the method used is to inculcate a password policy which comprises a minimum length, distorted words, and frequent alterations.

The recovery of the password is generally carried out by continual guessing of the password by using a computer algorithm. The computer repeatedly tries various combinations until the successful discovery of the password.

Eavesdropping Attack

These attacks initiate with the interference of network traffic. Another term used for Eavesdropping breach is sniffing or snooping. It is a type of a **network security attack** where the attacker attempts to steal the data send or received by computers, smartphones, or other digital devices. Eavesdropping attacks are hard to detect as they do not cause anomalous data transmissions.

Eavesdropping attacks aim at faded transmissions amid the server and the client, which allows the attacker to obtain network transmissions. Different network monitors such as sniffers on a server can be installed by the attacker to implement an eavesdropping attack and intercept data. Any device which is inside the transmission and reception network is a vulnerability point, including the initial as well as terminal devices. One method to guard against such attacks is having the information of devices connected to a specific network as well as information about software running on such devices.

Brute-Force and Dictionary Network Attacks

Brute-force and dictionary attacks are networking attacks in which an attacker tries to log into account of the user through systematically checking and exasperating all likely passwords until he finds the correct one.

The ordinary way to carry out this type of attack is through the front door, as we must have a technique of logging in. If we have the necessary credentials, we can enter as a normal user without arising doubtful logs, or tripping IDS signatures, or requiring an unpatched entry.

The meaning of brute-force is to overpower the system via repetition. During password hacking, brute force needs dictionary software, which combines dictionary words with hundreds of diverse variations. This process is rather slow. Brute-force dictionary attacks can make 100 to 1000 attempts per minute.

 After trying for numerous hours or even days, such attacks can finally crack any password. These attacks restate the significance of best practices of passwords, particularly on critical resources like routers, network switches, and servers.

Insider Threats

An attack doesn't need to be always performed by someone from outside an organization. At times, malicious attacks are carried out on a network or computer system by any individual sanctioned to access the system. Insiders executing such attacks have the advantage over outsider attackers as they have authorized system access. Moreover, they are most likely to understand network architecture and system policies.

Additionally, normally there is minor security against insider attacks as the focus of the majority of organizations is to defend themselves against external attacks. Insider threats can leave an impact on all elements of computer security. Such attacks can range from injecting Trojan viruses to thieving private information from a system or network.

Man-in-the-Middle (MITM) Attacks

Man-in-the-middle (abbreviated as MITM) attacks are a kind of cybersecurity breach permitting an attacker/ cracker to eavesdrop a communication amid two bodies. The attack takes place amid two genuinely communicating parties, allowing the attacker to capture communication, which they otherwise should not be able to access. This gives such attackers the name "man-in-the-middle." The invader "listens" to the communication through capturing the public key message transmission and then retransmits the key message whereas switching the demanded key with his own.

The two communicating parties continue to communicate routinely, without having any idea that the person who is sending messages is an unknown criminal who is trying to alter and access the message prior to its transmission to the receiver. Therefore, the intruder in this way controls the whole communication.

AI-Powered Attacks

The idea of a computer program learning on its own, constructing knowledge, and becoming more sophisticated in this process sounds scary (Adams 2017). We can easily dismiss artificial intelligence as another tech buzzword. Nevertheless, at present, it is being used in routinely applications with the help of an algorithmic process known as machine learning. Machine learning software aims to train a computer system to carry out a specific task on its own. Computers are trained to complete tasks by repeatedly doing them, whereby getting knowledge about particular hindrances that could hamper them.

Hackers can make use of artificial intelligence to hack into various systems such as autonomous drones and vehicles, altering them into prospective weapons. AI makes several cyber-attacks like password cracking, and denial-of-service attacks, identity theft, automatic, more efficient and powerful. AI can even be used to injure or murder people, or cause them emotional distress or steal their money. Attacks on a larger scale can affect national security, cut power supplies to complete districts, and may shut down hospitals as well.

Be Prepared For Attacks on Your Network

Previously, we have briefly reviewed the top cyber-security attack methods used by hackers for disturbing and compromising information systems. To install a good defense mechanism, we must first develop a good understanding of the offense. As we have seen, attackers have numerous available options while opting for attacks to disrupt and compromise information and computer systems. We also must adopt a proactive approach in securing our network and computer systems.

An updated antivirus database should be maintained. Workers must be trained, and passwords must be kept strong. Additionally, we can employ a low-privilege IT environment model to guard ourselves against cyber-attacks.

Security Countermeasures

External Measures

Currently, several nonprofit organizations are combating cyber-attacks. Examples include the International Association of Cybercrime Prevention (IACP) and Secure Domain Foundation (SDF) who are making efforts to make the individuals as well as companies conscious of the hazards, attacks, how they can be open to different types of cybercrime, and how they can guard themselves against such attacks. Besides such non-profit organizations, lately, Google has also initiated developing its own team, known as Project Zero, the purpose of which is to analyze susceptibilities and bugs in their own codes as well as in the codes of other companies to take all requisite steps for improving the software products to mitigate risks of cyber-attacks.

Financial institutions have also taken notice of the rising trend of cyber-attacks. One of the financial companies is AXA Corporate Solutions Company, which has launched an insurance product that covers the expenses required to recover after a cyber-attack, errors, viruses, or unintended events. Additionally, the company also introduced a product dedicated to analyzing, assessing and supporting mitigation of clients' cyber risks.

The legal aspect is a vital part of the discussion of cyber-crime and security. Different regulations and laws are constantly established for limiting or preventing cyber-crime; nevertheless, the fact is that each set of regulations and laws are geographically restricted to a particular area/ state etc.

Internal

No two companies are similar, which is why each company has its individual risk profile which depends on the size of the company, its business operating sector, and its geographical setup, etc. Each company must ensure carrying out a series of steps needed as preconditions for executing security controls, dealing with vulnerability points and identifying potential threats, to address the risks.

Companies must ensure the up-gradation of all essential equipment (e.g., software and hardware), especially data safety software (e.g., antivirus and anti-malware programs). It is also necessary for companies to ensure the agreement for software provided by a third party encompassing the upgrade and maintenance services. Other security controls

Contingent on the type of risks, numerous control mechanisms can be employed to ensure the integrity, availability, and confidentiality of data. Control mechanisms may vary from one corporation to another; these control systems can be categorized into the following classes:

i.   Detective controls: These types of control mechanisms are designed to detect threats to the information security;

ii. Preventive controls: These kinds of control mechanisms are aimed to prevent threats (e.g., access restriction to the enterprise's network);

iii. Corrective controls: These control mechanisms are aimed at correcting identified irregularities (e.g., data recovery after the cyber attack).

Chapter Four

Cybersecurity Types and Techniques

Introduction

Cybersecurity is the technique used to ensure the confidentiality, integrity, and availability of data. It is the ability to defend against and recovering from incidents such as power outages or hard drive failures, as well as guarding against attacks from adversaries. The latter term is composed of everyone from script kiddies to criminal groups and hackers who can execute advanced persistent threats (APTs), and pose grave risks to the enterprise. Just like network and application security is critical for cybersecurity. Likewise, important are disaster recovery planning and business continuity.

The security of any firm comes with a mandate from the company's senior management. The delicacy of the cyber world we now live in also stresses strong controls over cybersecurity. It is the responsibility of management to see that all systems are built to definite security standards, and that company workers are well trained.

The apprehension that a significant part of today's world depends on the internet should intrigue us to probe the following questions:

- How much of my private data is stored online?

- How much of my life is reliant on the internet?

- How much information about my customers is available through networks?

- How much of my business is reachable through networks?

With such a high level of reliance on computers, ignoring the prospect of cybercrime in one's business can be very risky and possibly detrimental to own self, one's business, employees, as well as customers.

Without a sagacity of security in our business, it is operating at a high risk of cyber-attacks.

Security Training

In any cybersecurity program, the weakest element is always the human. Cybersecurity begins with awareness—providing training to operations staff to implement a strong security stance, training code developers to develop secure codes, training end-users to identify social engineering attacks, and phishing emails.

Even if strong controls have been placed, even then, most of the companies will experience some type of cyber-attack. An invader will always look to exploit the weakest link, and numerous attacks can be easily prevented by just executing basic security tasks, also sometimes mentioned as "cyber hygiene." Just like a surgeon would never go in an operation room without first washing his hands; similarly, any company has a responsibility to implement the basic elements of cybersecurity care, for instance, adopting strong authentication practices and not keeping private data at openly accessible places.

However, a good cybersecurity strategy necessitates going further than these basics. Advanced hackers can evade the majority of defenses, and the attack surface — the number of techniques through which an attacker can gain access to a system — is expanding for most enterprises (Nagarajan et al. 2012). For instance, both our physical world and the information are merging, and nation-state detectives, as well as criminals, now pose a threat to the integrity, confidentiality, and availability of cyber-physical systems like medical devices, cars, power plants, even our internet of things (IoT) fridge. Likewise, the rising trend towards cloud computing, the internet of things (IoT), bring your own device (BYOD) policies in the office, are creating new challenges. Hence, it is more important than ever to defend all these systems.

The regulatory climate around the privacy of consumer even further complicates cybersecurity. Compliance with strict regulatory frameworks such as the European Union's General Data Protection Regulation (GDPR) stresses on adopting new types of roles to make sure that organizations meet the security and privacy mandates of the GDPR as well as other regulations.

Consequently, due to the increasing demand for cybersecurity professionals, hiring managers are making efforts to fill positions with capable candidates.

Tools and Techniques Employed in Cybersecurity

The security of any firm's IT environment is very critical. Every enterprise must take cybersecurity utterly seriously. Several hacking attacks affect businesses of all sizes. Few real security threats include malware, hackers, and viruses in the cyber world. Every company should be aware of the hazardous security attacks and must keep themselves secure. There are several characteristics of the cyber defense which must be considered. Below-mentioned are six essential services and tools which should be considered by every organization to ensure the strong measures of cybersecurity. These six tools are as under:

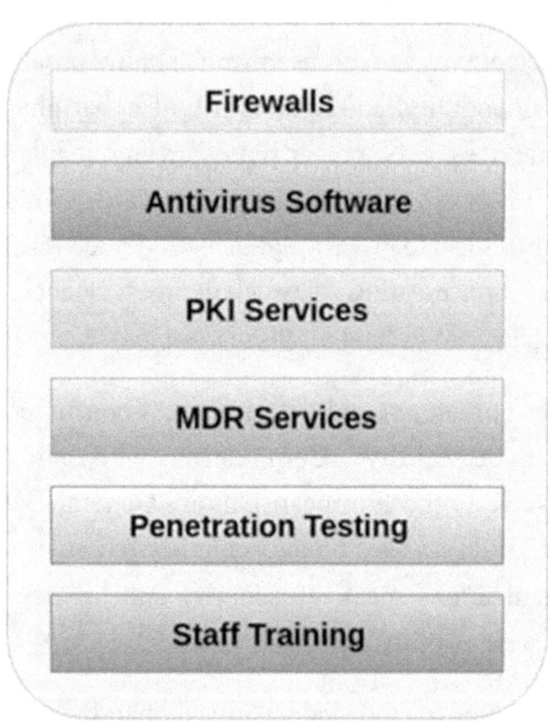

As we know that given the rising number of unsanctioned attempts to access private data, cybersecurity is now gaining eminence. The techniques and tools used for dealing with cybersecurity concerns are briefly described below:

PKI Services

Numerous people relate Public Key Infrastructure (PKI) only with TLS or SSL, the technology used for encrypting server communications and is responsible for the padlock and HTTPS we see in address bars of our browser (Wilson 2005). Though SSL is very significant, not merely for security of public sites but as well as for our internal networks, in reality, PKI can solve numerous common cybersecurity problems and deserves a place in security suite of each organization.

Besides server security, PKI can be used for other tasks as well; few are explained below:

Multi-Factor Authentication and Controlling Access

For security purposes, it must be ensured that only approved machines, users, and devices (those who have properly configured certificates) have the accessibility to operate on the company's networks. This basic technique of cybersecurity proposes to authenticate the identity of the user on the basis of the credentials stored in the security domain of the network system. Using a password is the most common mode of control; nevertheless, there are several other techniques, such as the insertion of the SIM card in anyone's mobile. SIM cards have distinct ID numbers which are passed through a protected communication line for identifying a certain mobile phone. The major encounter faced during the authenticating procedure is thwarting efforts of unsanctioned people who try to spy on the authenticating message. The password communicated through an insecure link is likely to be intercepted by fraudulent people who then can use it to camouflage as the original user. To solve this problem, we use encryption techniques.

Creation of Trusted Digital Signatures

Digital signatures confirm the identity of the signing person and make a tamper-evident seal for protecting the contents of the document and meeting compliance requirements.

Encryption of Email Messages and Verification of Identity of the Sender

Digital signatures and encryption all internal communication through emails reduce the chances of phishing and data loss hazards by clearly confirming the origin of the message so that receivers can identify genuine emails vs. phishing emails thereby, making sure that only intended addressees have access to the contents of the email. Encryption makes data inscrutable unless a proper key is applied for unlocking the data. To deal with encryption, an attacker would need to solve complex mathematical problems such as factorization of large primes requiring an astronomical quantity of computing resources as well as time. In symmetric encryption, the same key is used for both purposes of message encoding as well as message decoding, and the level of security is analogous to that of the key. Possible security dangers will accompany the dissemination of the key. In asymmetric encryption, a public key is used for encryption of the message; whereas, a private key is used for decryption of the same. Presently, most of the security protocols are using asymmetric encryption for the dissemination of keys.

Digital Signature and Code Protection

End-users must be assured that code is authentic and comes from a certified source. Additionally, code must be protected from tampering and the risks of malware injections. Digital signatures can be created out by using the same mathematical algorithms which are used in asymmetric encryption. A user can test to check that he has a private key by receiving some data encoded with it. The key will then verify the person's credentials. This process basically functions on the postulation that only the authorized user has access to the private key.

Building an Individuality and Trust in IoT Ecosystems

When we give a unique identity to each IoT device, it means they can authenticate when they come online thereby, proving their integrity throughout their lifespan, and securely communicating with other services, devices, and users.

Anti-Virus

In the present world, the threats of computer viruses or unwanted short programs triggering undesirable commands without taking the consent of the user are rising exponentially. There are two functions performed by anti-virus software; it stops installing of the virus in a system, and secondly, it scans the systems for viruses that have been already installed. The target of most viruses is the operating system of windows since it is the most favorite computing podium of masses. Even Linux, as well as Apple users, can also be attacked by viruses built exclusively for these operating systems.

If we are running a business but do not have much experience with cybersecurity, we might suppose that the terms 'antivirus' and 'firewall' are somewhat synonymous. However, they are not. For maintaining a secure system, it is crucial to have both, up-to-date antivirus software and a strong firewall in place. Both of these constitute vital components of our cybersecurity.

The function of antivirus software is to alert us to the presence of any virus and malware infections; several antivirus software also provide additional services like they can scan emails to make sure they are free from any malignant attachments or malicious web links. Current antivirus programs execute beneficial protective measures, for example, quarantining possible threats and eliminating them. A huge range of antivirus software are available in the market, and we can easily find a package according to the needs of our business.

Firewall

The purpose of a firewall is to effectually hamper any effort of unauthorized access to a computer system that is connected to the internet by hackers either directly or through other network connections. Firewalls come together with the majority of operating systems. Mostly, firewalls are turned on by default. We can take the aid of commercial firewalls if the level of security provided by the default firewall is not sturdy enough or if it is posturing interference to authentic network activities.

With the increasing sophistication of hacking techniques and resultant development of strong defenses, we might think that a firewall is outdated. However, this is not the case. A firewall is perhaps the most central of security tools, as it remains one of the most significant tools. A firewall can be implemented as software, hardware, or a combination of both hardware and software. The firewall aims to block any unauthorized access to our computer and network system. All messages leaving or entering the internet have to pass through the firewall, which first inspects each message and blocks those which do not fulfill the definite security criteria.

A firewall monitors both network traffic and connection attempts, determining whether or not these should be let pass easily onto a computer or network system. Firewalls are beneficial. However, they do have limitations. Expert hackers have learned the art of creating such programs and data which can trick firewalls into considering them trustworthy – which means that the program will be able to pass through the firewall without encountering any problem. In spite of these limitations, firewalls are still considered quite effective for the detection of the big majority of less advanced malicious attacks on businesses.

Managed Detection Services

With the sophistication of hackers and cyber-criminals and the advancement of the techniques as well as different software used by them, it has become indispensable for companies to capitalize on more powerful systems of defense. Now, it is not enough to have simple defenses that can react to threats – instead, companies should adopt a proactive approach and must identify attacks prior to them causing any problems.

Cybersecurity has experienced a gradual shift from financing techniques that attempt to avoid the risk of an attack towards advanced techniques which react to as well as to detect possible security concerns, and retort to them as quickly as possible. Obviously, it is far less harmful to recognize and eradicate an attack prior to it spreads instead of attempting to handle an attack that now already has a resilient foothold on one's IT network.

Penetration Testing

Penetration testing is a chief technique to test the security systems of one's business. During penetration testing, cybersecurity experts will employ similar techniques as used by criminal hackers for checking of any likely vulnerabilities and potential areas of weaknesses. A pen test aims to simulate the type of attack that might face by a business from criminal hackers, including everything from phishing to code injection and password cracking. After the conclusion of the test, the testers will present their observations and can thus provide help by recommending possible modifications to our system.

Staff Training

We might not consider staff training as a 'tool,' nonetheless, in the end, having educated employees who have a good understanding of their role in cybersecurity, can prove to be one of the strongest ways of defense against potential attacks. Several training tools are available in the market which can be used for educating the company's staff about the best prevalent practices of cybersecurity.

Even trivial techniques such as regular updates on strategies of cybersecurity and adopting the right practices of passwords can create a huge difference. Another smart way is to arrange simulations or training sessions that can educate to identify con emails or suspicious links, which might be a part of a phishing attack. The strength of our defenses does not matter if the company staff can be tricked via social engineering schemes.

With the increase in the sophistication level of methods used by cyber-criminals, companies must invest in such tools and services. Failing to do that can leave a company in a position where it becomes an easy target for criminal hackers. The expenditure of the required investment might put company owners off, but it must be remembered that this initial investment will reward the company's business with long-term protection and security .

Types of Cybersecurity

The cybersecurity has a very broad scope. The core areas of cybersecurity are described as under. A good cybersecurity strategy will take all of these areas into account.

Critical Infrastructure

Critical infrastructure comprises the cyber-physical systems upon which society relies, such as purification of water, the electricity grid, traffic lights, and hospitals. For instance, plugging the internet to a power plant makes it defenseless against cyber-attacks. Organizations in charge of critical infrastructure must perform their work with due diligence to protect infrastructure and must have a thorough understanding of the susceptibilities and guard against them. The security of this critical infrastructure is very important for the safety of our society. Everyone else ought to evaluate the effect on critical infrastructure, which such an attack might cause, and then develop a contingency plan. Few common examples of critical infrastructure are mentioned below:

    i.   electricity grid

    ii. traffic lights

    iii. purification of water

    iv. hospitals

    v. shopping centers

Organizations which are not in control for critical infrastructure, but depends on it for a share of their business, must create an emergency plan by assessing how such an attack carried on critical infrastructure might affect them.

Network Security

Network security protects against unsanctioned invasion and malicious insiders. However, safeguarding network security usually entails trade-offs. For instance, access controls like extra logins might be needed, but they decelerate productivity.

Tools that are employed for monitoring network security produce a lot of data — to the extent that genuine warnings are often missed. To manage monitoring of network security in a better way, security teams are now gradually making use of machine learning to flag anomalous traffic and being vigilant to threats in real-time. Network security makes sure the security of internal networks by safeguarding the infrastructure and preventing unauthorized access to it (Chen, Paxon and Katz 2010). Network administrators keep on developing and implementing such procedures and policies for preventing unapproved access, alteration, and exploitation of the network.

Few common examples of implementation of network security are stated below:

    i. New passwords

    ii. application security

    iii. extra logins

    iv. encryption

v. Monitored internet access

vi. antivirus programs

vii. firewalls

viii. antispyware software

Cloud Security

Whenever any organization moves into the cloud world, it generates new security challenges for it. For instance, in 2017, data breaches were reported almost weekly from poorly configured cloud cases. Even though cloud providers are constantly creating and developing novel security tools for helping company users to secure their data in a better way, still the bottom line persists: when it comes to cybersecurity, moving to the cloud is not a complete solution for accomplishing due diligence. Improved and advanced cybersecurity is one of the major explanations why the cloud is taking succession.

Cloud security is a security tool based on software and monitors, as well as protects the data in our cloud resources. There is a wrong perception of cloud computing that it's not as secure as traditional methods. Most people consider that their data is more protected when it is stored on physical systems and servers which are owned and controlled by them which is not the case as security and accessibility of data do not merely depend on the physical location of the data.

A report on cloud security stated that on-premises environment users undergo more cases as compared to those of service provider environments.

It was further stated in the report that:

i. Roughly 61.4 attacks are experienced by on-premise environment users whereas;

ii. Service provider environment users experienced approximately 27.8 attacks on average.

Cloud computing security is analogous to conventional methods on-premise data centers, the advantage is that it saves both cost and time of maintaining giant data facilities; moreover, the threat of security breaches is marginal.

Application Security

Application security, particularly web application security, has to turn into the most fragile technical attack point. However, few enterprises manage to reduce all the vulnerabilities sufficiently. Application security instigates with secure coding practices and must be augmented through penetration testing.

Prompt application development, as well as deployment to the cloud world, has resulted in the introduction of a new discipline, which is development and operations (DevOps). Development and operations teams generally prioritize business requirements over security, a trend that will probably change, given the propagation of threats.

Application security must be opted as one of the many required security measures adopted by companies to protect their systems. Application security makes use of both hardware and software methods to deal with external threats that can ensue during the development stage of an application.

It is easier to access applications over networks, resulting in the implementation of security measures during the development stage to be a vital stage of the project.

Different types of application security are mentioned below:

i. Firewalls

ii. antivirus programs

iii. encryption programs

These types of application security help to prevent unauthorized access to systems. Companies can also identify their sensitive data possessions and guard them by using particular application security procedures attached to such data sets.

Internet of Things (IoT) Security

IoT denotes to an extensive range of both critical as well as non-critical cyber-physical systems such as sensors, printers, electronic appliances, and security cameras. It is common by IoT devices to ship in an insecure state, and most of the devices do not offer significant security patching, which not only poses threats just to their users but to other people on the internet as well since such devices usually find themselves part of a botnet. As a result, unique security challenges are to be faced both by home users as well as society.

According to professionals:

i. By 2021, it is anticipated that the combined markets of IoT will propagate to around $520 billion which is more than double than the year 2017 where market was around $235 billion;

ii. The fundamental technology of the IoT market includes IoT's data center, consumer devices, analytics, legacy embedded systems, networks, and connectors.

iii. IoT devices often get into vulnerable states offering little to almost no security patching, thereby posing a unique security challenge for its users.

A study carried out by Bain stated that

i. One of the main hurdles in adopting IoT is security challenges associated with it.

ii. Companies would purchase more IoT devices regularly provided security concerns are addressed

iii. Most enterprises expect that the business of IoT will expand in the future to a great extent.

This demands from sellers to make investments in getting extensive knowledge about security challenges so that more strategic solutions can be proposed as well as implemented. IoT devices have nearly become impossible to avoid, and thus, our best option will be to find an IT provider who can well manage their security

Common Cyber Threats

There are three general categories of common cyber threats categories (Abomhara 2015):

1. Attacks on confidentiality

2. Attacks on integrity

3. Attacks on availability

4. Social engineering

5. Phishing attacks

6. Unpatched software

7. Social media threats

8. Advanced persistent threats

Chapter Five

Network Security and Security of Complex Infrastructures

Introduction

The consumption of the internet is rising exponentially, hence, making the security of network more vital with each passing day. Quite often, the data flow faces numerous problems. The data is sometimes altered, corrupted, lost or even fabricated. People using the internet naturally have some expectation among which integrity and confidentiality of data are their topmost concerns. If someone using the internet receives any message, he /she will want to identify the message sender so that in any situation, if the sender negates sending the message, then they can provide evidence to prove him wrong.

The term 'Industrial Control System' (ICS) talks about a group of process automation techniques, like Distributed Control Systems (DCS), and Supervisory Control and Data Acquisition (SCADA) systems which unluckily have been the target of increasing number of attacks from the past few years. Since these systems provide crucial services to critical infrastructure like communications, energy, and manufacturing services, increasing attacks by intimidating intruders pose a serious threat to the routine running of nation-states.

ICS have distinct reliability as well as performance requirements and habitually use operating systems, applications, and techniques that might not be considered conventional by current IT professionals. Generally, these requirements follow the precedence of availability and integrity, succeeded by confidentiality and take into account the management of processes which, in case of not implemented properly, present a significant threat to the safety and health of human lives, harm the environment, as well as results in severe financial problems like production losses. Additionally, the unavailability of critical infrastructure (such as transport, electrical power) can result in such economic effect which is far beyond the systems bearing direct and physical damage. Such economic impacts can lead to harmful effects on the local, provincial, national, or even global economy.

Network Security Requirements

With the internet has come the ability to connect any computer from anywhere in the world to any other computer placed at any other location in the world. This is both a blessing and a nightmare. For people at home, surfing on the internet is entertainment. However, for corporate security managers, it can be a nightmare. Many companies have a huge quantity of confidential data on-line such as product development plans, marketing strategies, trade secrets, financial analysis, etc. The release of such sensitive information to an opponent/ competitor can have dreadful consequences. Besides risks of data being leaked out, there is another risk as well which is of information/ data being leaked in. Especially, worms, viruses, and several other digital pests can attempt to breach the security of the system, destroy the treasured data as well as a waste of a huge amount of time of database administrator for cleaning up the mess.

Due to security concerns, government and commercial enterprises are hesitant to use the internet. For the past few years, numerous attacks on routers have been reported. Presently, the internet uses Border Gateway Protocol (BGP) for inter-domain routing. Moreover, since BGP sessions employ TCP for transmission of data amid routers, the latest rise in TCP based attacks have become a further threat to the security of BGP. Earlier, SNMP (Simple Network Management Protocols) were used by the internet community for monitoring network health and debugging operational problems.

Objectives of Data Security

The main responsibility of data security is to secure the systems from following threats:

Interception

The unsanctioned person gains access to the system for capturing the data in the network. The security against interception must be ensured for the confidentiality of data.

Modification

The unsanctioned person can modify the data in the network after gaining unauthorized access to the system. The defense against any such modification is necessary for maintaining the integrity of the data.

Fabrication

The unsanctioned person inset bogus data in-network or can add records in the stored files. To guard against fabrication is requisite for authentication of the data.

Interruption

Complete data or some parts of it are destroyed. The guard is to save the data from such interruption.

Non-Repudiation

Both data sender and recipient are proscribed from negating any data which is sent or received, which means that the recipient must be able to provide proof that a particular message came from some source.

Table Error! No text of specified style in document.-2. Key stakeholders who pose a threat to the security of data

Adversary	Goal
Student	Snooping on people's e-mail for fun
Cracker	Stealing data to test out security system of anyone
Sales rep	for claiming to represent all of Europe not just a single country
Businessman	for discovering the strategic marketing plan of a competitor
Ex-employee	For getting revenge for being fired
Accountant	To steal money from an enterprise

Stockbroker	To repudiate a promise made to a client through e-mail
Con man	for stealing credit card numbers for sale
Spy	for learning military or commercial secrets of an enemy
Terrorist	for stealing germ warfare secrets

Internet Security Techniques

Below mentioned are five main types of internet security techniques:

1. Cryptography

2. Firewall

3. Disconnecting when not in usage

4. Protocols

5. Not opening unknown email attachments

Cryptography

The meaning of the word cryptography is 'Secret Writing.' It can deliver confidentiality, integrity, as well as authentication and non-repudiation of messages. Cryptography uses two techniques which are Encryption and Decryption. The message which needs encryption is called plaintext which is transferred into ciphertext using a key as a parameter. The path of cryptography is as below:

Plain text > Encryption > Ciphertext > Decryption > Plain text

Here,

i. The transformation of plain text to ciphertext is Encryption.

ii. After encryption, the transformed message is known as ciphertext.

iii. Transformation of the ciphertext back into plain text is decryption.

Plain text is the original message prior to being transformed, whereas ciphertext is the transformed message. Hence the message which needs to be sent is converted into a distinct message through encryption. The intruder does not know the key and therefore duplicates the ciphertext. The function key is only known to the user/recipient. Thus, only he can transform the ciphertext back into plain text through the decryption process. In this way, cryptography helps to maintain the security of data.

Firewall

Firewall plays the role of a gatekeeper amid the outside world and the internal network of the company. The firewall performs as an electronic barrier for stopping unauthorized entries. Principally, it performs two significant functions which are:

Gatekeeping

Firewall inspects the location from where the data tries to enter in our system and then based on instructions, elects, whether or not to permit entry of that data.

Monitoring

Another function of a firewall is to monitor information. It monitors logging of all system activities as well as the generation of reports for system administration. Monitoring is of two types, i.e., active and passive.

When an event takes place during active monitoring, firewall directs information about the event to the manager. Whereas, in the case of passive monitoring, the firewall makes records of details of each event on a disk. The manager keeps checking those details after regular intervals and marks results. Network Firewalls (both hardware and software-based) delivers some level of protection against attacks of intruders.

Architecture of Firewall

Any enterprise connected to the internet through a serial line might opt to connect a firewall, as presented in the following figure.

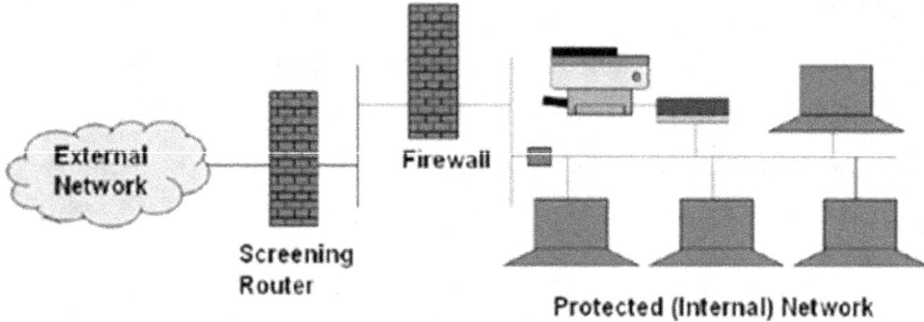

Firewall offers an appropriate point for monitoring of internet security.

Disadvantages of Firewalls

An internet firewall is unable to protect against attacks which do not come through the firewall. Moreover, it cannot guard against transferring virus, which might take place through infected files or software. Firewall further cannot defend against threats due to corporate spies from replicating confidential data onto a disk. Besides, it cannot shield against data-driven attacks which take place when unobjectionable data is copied or mailed to an internal host and used for launching an attack.

Disconnecting When Not In Use

The users must disconnect from the internet when they are not using it. An intruder/hacker cannot attack a computer that is powered off or not connected to the internet, thus disconnecting from the network while not using is recommended.

Protocols

Use some standardized set of protocols designed for providing the security of a network. For example, WEP Protocol provided by 802.11 standards is used for the security of a wireless LAN.

Opening an Unknown Email Attachment

Prior to opening any email attachment, we must ensure the source of the attachment. Melissa virus can even initiate from a known address. An e-mail sent through a network is similar to a postcard that can be read by anyone who has the skill to lay hands on it. For ensuring secrecy of message, both the sender and recipient must agree on a secret key.

Another method of safeguarding the e-mail message outside the network is by using the practice known as signing a message. Prior to opening an attachment and authentication of its source, the following steps are suggested to carry out.

i. Save the file to hard disk.

ii. Scan the file using anti-virus software.

iii. After scanning the file, open it. Following these simple steps can decrease the spreading of malicious code, which might be present in the attachment.

Cybersecurity of Critical Infrastructures

Regardless of the seeming risks associated with critical infrastructure, still, the security of industrial control systems (ICS) systems is not considered a significant investment area. Naedele (2007) claims that the expenses associated with the security of ICS are excessive, particularly in case of critical systems, when we cannot quantify the alleged risks to an enterprise or infrastructure, and a business case cannot be adequately articulated. Quite often, this results in an immature incident response-ability in the installed operative ICS, particularly within the SME (Small and medium-sized enterprises) supply chain. Larger infrastructures, on the other hand, suffer from the inadequate understanding of the deployed apparatuses like Intelligent Electronic Devices (IED) or Programmable Logic Controllers (PLC), Remote Terminal Units (RTU) and input/output (I/O) devices which are employed for managing electromechanical tools in either local or else distributed environments. This particular environment which pools big scale, geographically scattered, proprietary system components, offers major challenges to SOCs (Security Operation Centers) as well as to Cyber Emergency Response Teams.

Earlier, ICS were functioned as detached networks not connected to any public communication infrastructures; however, with the expansion of businesses using the data and services delivered through the Internet, such isolation that guarded these systems has reduced. The advantages provided by real-time monitoring, numerous sessions, concurrency, peer to peer communications, maintenance and redundancy have greatly improved the services provided for both operators and consumers. Furthermore, this interconnectedness is expected to increase with the execution of smart grids and implementation of the Internet of Things (IoT). Therefore, the formerly isolated systems are becoming more and more exposed to a variety of risks (Tzokatziou, Maglaras and Janicke). Apropos which, Byres, Eng and Fellow (2012) have cited that previously isolated ICS have now 11 direct connections on average across networks with frail network segmentation.

The focus of IT safety is normally to protect networked computer assets having shared attributes. However, Zhu, Joseph, and Sastry (2011) debated that the security of ICS requires a combination of traditional computer security as well as communication networking with control engineering. However, due to limitations of conventional IT security, control systems security and communications security, the efficiency of security of present ICS systems is still to be proven. Luallen (2015) reported observations of a survey conducted with 268 respondent organizations out of which most did not report precarious ICS assets and depended on their employees to identify issues, not tools.

SCADA Systems

SCADA (Supervisory Control and Data Acquisition) systems have customarily been linked with a subset of ICS known as Wide Area Control systems.

The security of these systems is more significant as compared to the majority of other computer systems due to the potential sternness of the consequences which degrading of service might cause, as well as the disturbance to routine life. With earlier computer systems, the key concern was not security but reliability. These days, due to greater connectivity, security is high on the priority list. Additionally, SCADA systems are becoming increasingly connected to the internet, and the communications in them take place over shared Internet Protocol (IP) infrastructure.

Present research states several concerns related to the implementation of security in SCADA systems:

i   The reliability of a system often takes preference over security threats and can lead to high-security susceptibility.

ii   No encryption in formerly used communication protocols (often plain text is used).

iii The commonly utilized well-documented protocols, as well as off the shelf hardware solutions, can impend to destabilize obscurity (Nicholson 2012) as a result of which attacking can become easier.

iv The SCADA operation needs to be continuous, which makes the application of updates and performing patching or modifying system components quiet difficult.

v The long life of today's systems as compared to the systems in the past signifies that software and hardware are operating past their supported life expectancy.

The above-mentioned explicit characteristics and restrictions associated with SCADA imply the need for a domain-specific approach. In-line security setups such as conventional network IDS application or security tools at the host level, such as anti-virus, are not suggested due to likely latency effect or the incidents of single points of failure along the essential communications route. Moreover, with the aggregating sophistication of cyber-attacks, cyber-security can no longer rely on controlled, pattern-based detection algorithms for assuring constant security monitoring. Approaches must be adopted which can handle rogue risks and offer a more appropriate balance amid detection and maintenance power.

Real-World Attacks

STUXNET is a sophisticated computer worm infection and perfectly embodies an example of the weakness of the regulatory systems dedicated to controlling critical infrastructures (McMillan 2010). Initially insulated in June of 2010, the STUXNET computer virus was particularly designed to attack Windows-based industrial computers as well as to take control of Programmable Logic Controller (PLCs). The virus accomplished this task by impelling the behavior of remote actuators, which lead to instability phenomena. The enigma is that critical infrastructures immensely depends on the latest interconnected (and susceptible) ICT (Information and Communication) technologies, whereas the control apparatus is generally old. These factors can result in grave circumstances by exposing the systems to a wide variety of attacks.

The lesson learned from the spread of the STUXNET worm is that to deal with a particular low-level threat in an effective manner, both the global and local perspectives should be considered. As a matter of fact, in addition to gaining a broader standpoint on the state of the Systems, the intelligence of equipment, as well as devices (used for influencing the behavior of the system, for instance, valves, RTUs, etc.) should be increased.

Another method used by cyber-attackers for paralyzing a SCADA system is by saturating the bandwidth of the carrier utilized for the communication. This approach was used by the SLAMMER worm in 2003 to disturb the SCADA of two utilities as well as a nuclear power plant of the United States. According to ANSI/ISA.99 (American National Standards Institute/ International Society of Automation), availability is the most significant feature of information security. The absence of information to/from the field in a timely fashion might result in intense consequences since when the field is incapable of receiving the suitable command, then even small episodes may also result in provoking dramatic effects, as was the case of the US black-out.

A case of the Mariposa botnet infection in an ICS company was investigated by the US Department of Homeland Security, which described that the reason the infection occurred was that a worker used a USB drive for downloading presentation materials to a business laptop. As soon as the employee connected the company laptop to the corporate network, the virus spread to more than 100 hosts.

Another reason for the increasing complexity associated with the security of SCADA communications is the decision to link IT networks with the SCADA networks to permit faster and better communications. However, these advanced characteristics have amplified the threats and hazards of SCADA communications. Presently, there are not any definite solutions to implement the security of SCADA communications in that outlook. Several EU projects like the FP7 CRUTIAL (Critical Utility Infrastructural Resilience) and FP6 SAFEGUARD have worked on the technical feasibility for improving the cybersecurity of the SCADA system through refining the intelligence of the field devices.

Chapter Six

Introduction to Security Testing

Introduction

Security testing is the process that is executed with the target of revealing imperfections in the security mechanisms and discovering the weaknesses or vulnerabilities of software applications. Recent breaches of the security systems at retailers like **Home Depot and Target**, along with **Apple Pay** competitor **Current C**, emphasize the significance of confirming that the efforts of security testing are up to date.

The main goal of security testing is to discover how defenseless a security system might be and to decide whether its resources and data are secured from potential intruders. Online transactions have rapidly increased in late making security testing as the most crucial areas of testing for web applications. Security testing is more efficient in recognizing potential vulnerabilities when executing regularly.

Generally, the following attributes are associated with security testing:

    i. Authentication

    ii. Confidentiality

iii. Authorization

iv. Availability

v. Non-repudiation

vi. Integrity

vii. Resilience

Need for the Security Testing

In the present scenario security testing is very critical to recognize and look after web application security vulnerabilities to avert any of the following:

i.   Loss of customer trust.

ii. Website downtime, expenditures and time loss in improving from damage (restoring backups, reinstalling services, etc.)

iii. Disturbance to the online means of income generation/collection.

iv. Cost related to securing web applications against future attacks.

v.   Associated fees and legal implications for having careless security measures in the place.

Classes of Threats

Discussed below are the different kinds of threats that are or can be utilized to take benefit of the security vulnerability.

Privilege Elevation

Privilege elevation is the class or type of attack where the hacker generally has an account on the system and utilizes it to increase the privileges of his system to the higher level than she/he wasn't meant to have. If fruitful, this class of attack can outcome in a hacker attaining privileges as high as root on the UNIX system. Once the hacker obtains super-user privileges, she/he can execute code with this high level of privilege, and the complete system is efficiently compromised .

SQL Injection

An SQL injection is the usual application layer attack method used by the hackers, in which malicious SQL (Structured Query Language) statements are introduced into the entry field for implementation. The attacks of SQL injection are very crucial as the attacker can obtain precarious information from the server database. It is a kind of attack which obtains the benefit of loopholes existent in the execution of web applications that permits the hacker to hack the entire system. To check the attack of SQL injection input fields like comments, text boxes, etc. need to be taken care of. To avert injections, special characters must be either skipped or properly handled from the input.

Unauthorized Data Access

One of the most popular kinds of attacks is obtaining unauthorized access to the data within an application. Data can usually be accessed on a network or on servers (Deo 1997).

Unauthorized access comprises:

i. Unauthorized access to the data through data-fetching operations

ii. Unauthorized access to the reusable client verification information by observing the access of others

iii. Unauthorized access to the data by observing the access of others

URL Manipulation

URL manipulation is a process of controlling the website URL (Uniform Resource Locater) query strings and capture of the significant information by hackers. This takes place when the application utilizes the HTTP GET technique to pass information amongst the server and client. The information is usually passed in the parameters in the query string. The tester can alter the value of the parameter in the query string to confirm if the server approves it.

DoS (Denial of Service)

A DoS attack is an obvious effort to make a network or machine resource unavailable to legitimate users. Applications can also be breached in ways that make the application and, at times, the complete machine, unusable.

Data Manipulation

In data manipulation, the hacker alters data used by the website to gain some benefit or embarrass the owners of the website. Hackers will frequently gain access to HTML (Hypertext Markup Language) pages and alter them to be offensive or satirical.

Identity Spoofing

Identity spoofing is a method where the hacker utilizes the credentials of the legitimate device or user to start attacks against the network hosts, bypass access controls, or steal data. Preventing this attack needs network-level mitigations and IT-infrastructure

Cross-Site Scripting (XSS)

Cross-site scripting (XSS) is the computer security vulnerability discovered in web applications. Cross-site scripting enables the attackers to introduce a client-side script into the Web pages seen by the other users and trick the user into clicking on that particular URL. Once performed by the user's browser, this script or code could then execute actions like entirely changing the behavior of the website, thieving personal data, or executing actions on behalf of the user. All attacks listed above are the most critical threat types, but these aren't all. The graph below explains the percentage (%) of some well-known cyber-attacks.

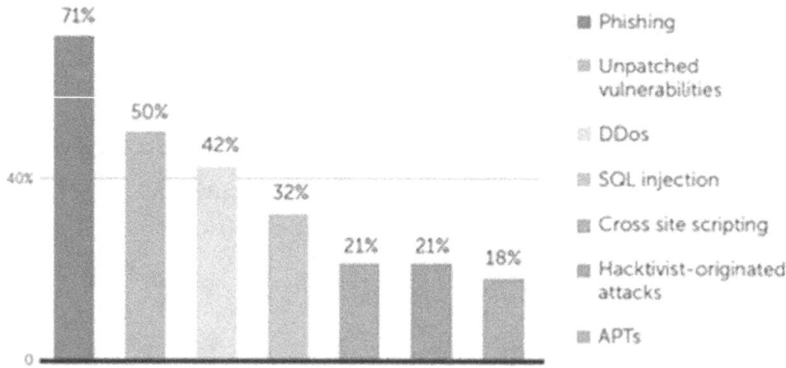

Security Testing Techniques

To avoid the security mentioned above testing flaws/threats and implement security testing on the web application, it is needed to have sound knowledge of HTTP (Hypertext Transfer Protocol) and a good understanding of client-server communication via HTTP. Also, fundamental knowledge of XSS and SQL injection is required. The following methods will help in executing quality security testing:

Cross-Site Scripting (XSS)

The tester should, also, check the web application for Cross-site scripting. Any script e.g. <SCRIPT> or any HTML e.g. <HTML> should not be acknowledged by the application. If it is, then the application can be inclined to an attack by XSS (Cross-Site Scripting).

Attackers can utilize this method to implement malicious scripts or URLs on the victim's browser. Using cross-site scripting (XSS) attackers can utilize scripts like JavaScript to steal user cookies and the information saved in the cookies. XSS (Cross-Site Scripting) Testing can normally be done for:

i.   Apostrophe

ii. Less-Than Sign

iii. Greater-Than Sign

Ethical Hacking

Ethical hacking means the hacking performed by an individual or a company to help recognize possible threats on a network or computer. An ethical hacker tries to bypass the security of the system and look for any loophole that could be misused by the malicious hackers, aka the Black hats. White hats might suggest changes to the systems that make the system less probable to be breached by black hats (Palmer 2001).

Password Cracking

This is the most crucial part while performing system testing. To gain access to the reserved areas of the applications, hackers can utilize the password cracking tool or usually can guess the common password. Common passwords or usernames are effortlessly available online, along with the open-source password cracking applications. Until the web application applies the complex password, it is very simple to crack the password and username. Another method of cracking the passwords is if a password/username is to aim cookies if the cookies are saved without encryption.

Penetration Testing

This is an attack on the computer system to locate security loopholes, possibly gaining access to the system, its data, and functionality.

Risk Assessment

This is the process of evaluating and concluding on the risk indulged with the kind of loss and the probability of vulnerability occurrence. This is decided within the organization by numerous interviews, analyses, and discussions.

Security Auditing

This is the systematic evaluation of the security of the company's information system by assessing how well it obeys to the set of developed criteria.

Security Scanning

Security scanning is a program that usually communicates with the web application via web front-end to recognize potential security loopholes in the web application, Networks, and OS.

SQL Injection Check

The next thing which needs to be checked is the SQL injection. Entering the single quote (') in the textbox must be disallowed by the application. Instead, if the tester comes across a database error, it generally means that the user input is injected in some query and then implemented by the application. In such a situation, the application is susceptible to SQL injection.

The attacks of SQL injection are very critical as the attackers can obtain critical information from the database of the server. To check the SQL injection entry points into the web application, discover code from the code base where MySQL queries are implemented on the server database by taking some user inputs.

SQL Injection Testing can usually be done for:

    i.   Apostrophes

    ii.   Commas

    iii. Brackets

    iv. Quotation marks

Vulnerability Scanning

This is the automated computer program to proactively recognize the security vulnerabilities of the computing systems in the network. This is used to determine where the system can be threatened and/or exploited.

Posture Assessment

This describes the complete security posture of the organization; it is the combination of Security scanning, Ethical hacking, and Risk Assessment.

URL Manipulation Via HTTP GET Methods

HTTP GET technique is used between server and application client to convey the information. The tester verifies if the application is conveying important information in a query string. The information through HTTP is passed in the parameters in the query string. To test this, a value of the parameter can be altered in the query string to validate if the server admits it.

Normally user information is passed via HTTP GET request to a server for either fetching data or authentication. Hackers can control the input of GET request to the server so that the needed information can be collected or corrupting the data. Any unexpected behavior of a web server or application, in such circumstances, is vital for the hacker to slide into the application.

Ad hoc Data Testing is an important part of security testing:

    i.   Random data, comprised of the requests, is tested.

   ii.   Random data, comprised of parameters, is tested.

iii. Random encoded data, comprised of parameters, is tested.

Buffer Overflow Testing

This type of testing possesses the following characteristics:

i. The string lengths, i.e., 1024 bytes, 256 bytes, 128 bytes, are put through boundary value testing

ii. Long, single-character strings

iii. Variable patterns of strings

Security Testing Approach

We can follow the next approach while we plan and prepare for the security test:

i. Security Architecture Study: The main step is in understanding the security goals, business requirements, and goals as far as organizational security compliance goes. When you plan for the test, you must consider every security factor the organization may have considered for accomplishing PCI compliance.

ii. Security Architecture Analysis: Know and then analyze the necessities of an application when it is being tested.

iii. Classify Security Testing: Gather all of the information about the system setup utilized for the development of the networks and software, such as technology, Operating Systems, hardware. List the Security Risks and Vulnerabilities.

iv. Threat Modeling: Based on the step above, prepare the Threat profile.

v. Test Planning: Based on the identified Threat, Security Risks and Vulnerabilities prepare test plans so the problems can be addressed.

vi. Traceability Matrix Preparation: For every identified Threat, Security Risks and Vulnerabilities prepare Traceability Matrix.

vii. Security Testing Tool identification: We cannot implement every security test manually, so the tool must be classified to ensure the security tests are fast and reliable.

viii. Test Case Preparation: Prepare the document of the Security test case.

ix. Test Case Execution: Implement the Security Test case performance and ensure all fixes are retested. Implement the Regression Test cases.

x. Reports: Prepare a comprehensive report of the Security Testing, which includes Threats and Vulnerabilities contained, detailing threats, and problems that remain open, etc.

Security Test Tools

This is a small number of the tools available for web application security testing (Curphey and Arawo 2006; Gu, Yin-Sheng, and You-yuan 2010; Garg 2016).

BeFF

The Browser Exploitation Framework tool is for web browsers – it takes benefit of cracking into open web browser designs, target the system, and move on.

BFB Tester

BFB Tester is a binary program security tool. BFB Tester will execute checks of multiple and single environment variable overflows, and argument command line overflows. It is used for warning security professionals of the programs utilizing unsafe temp file names by monitoring for the temp file creation activity.

Brakeman

This is usually an open-source susceptibility scanner that is made for Ruby on the Rails applications. The Rails application code is statically analyzed to discover security concerns, wherever they may occur in the development.

CROSS

The Codenomicon Robust Open Source Software (CROSS) program is made to assist open source projects that are part of the internet infrastructure, and repair critical code errors. The CROSS line of products is a suite of tools for testing network protocols. These are known as DEFENSICS, which assist the projects to find and repair lots of crucial flaws very quickly.

Ettercap

Ettercap is a free, open-source, and network security tool for man-in-the-middle attacks on LAN. This can be used in security auditing to test network protocols.

Flawfinder

This program scans C and C++ source code, reporting any potential threats. The default setting is to place the reports in order of risk level.

Gendarmerie

Gendarmerie is a rule-centered tool that is extensible, and is used or locating problems in .NET libraries and applications. It inspects libraries and programs that comprise code in the ECMA CIL format and searches for common issues in code, issues that compilers don't normally check, or haven't historically checked.

Knock

This is an efficient scanning tool to scan the subdomains and is also used for discovering transfer zones and testing wildcards, using an external or internal wordlist. This tool is quite helpful in the black box penetration test to discover vulnerable subdomains.

Metasploit Framework

This platform is open-source and an advanced tool for making, testing, and utilizing exploit code. It was primarily started as nothing more than a portable game but, over time, has advanced and is now one of the most powerful tools for vulnerability research, exploit development, and penetration testing,

Nessus

This is a world-leading vulnerability scanner with configuration auditing, high-speed and sensitive data discovery, asset profiling and security vulnerability analysis. You can disseminate Nessus scanners throughout the complete enterprise, inside the DMZs, and across all physical networks.

Paros

This is a Java-based HTTPS/HTTP proxy for assessing the web application vulnerability. All HTTPS and HTTP data between client and server, including form fields and cookies, can be interrupted and altered using these scanners.

Nikto

This is another open-source scanner for web servers, specifically to detect obsolete software configurations, invalid CGIs or data, etc. Comprehensive tests are executed over and again against the web servers.

Nmap

Network Mapper is an open-source scanner for security auditing and network discovery. Nmap utilizes raw IP packets to determine the hosts that may be available on a network, what services those hosts are providing, what OS versions and operating systems are being run, the packet firewalls/filters in utilization, etc

Skipfish

This is an active web application susceptibility security scanning tool. Security professionals utilize this tool to scan the sites for vulnerabilities. Reports produced by this tool serve as a basis for the professional web application security assessments.

Nsiqcppstyle

Nsiqcppstyle offers easy, extensible, sustainable code checking for C and C++ code. The analysis engine is isolated, along with the rules and the users can make their own C/C++ coding rules. Not only that, the rule server is customizable.

SET (Social-Engineer Toolkit)

Open-source, the idea behind SET is that the attacks are directed at human elements instead of system elements, enabling users to send java applets, emails, etc.

Oedipus

This is also an open-source web application testing suite and security analysis written in Ruby. It is skilled in parsing different kinds of log files off-line and recognizing security vulnerabilities. Utilizing the analyzed information, this can vigorously test web sites for web server and application vulnerabilities.

Vega

An open-source GUI-based tool, Vega is a multi-platform web security tool that is utilized to find examples of SQL injection, XSS (cross-site scripting), and web application susceptibilities. Vega also debugs web applications using an intercepting proxy. JavaScript is typically used in writing Vega attack models, and users can easily alter them or can write their own.

Wire Shark

Wire shark, formerly known as Ethereal, is the network packet analyzer. The network professionals around the globe utilize it for analysis, troubleshooting, protocol, and software development.

ZAP

The Zed Attack Proxy ZAP is a simple to use assimilated penetration testing tool for locating vulnerabilities in the web applications. It is developed to be utilized by people with a broad range of security experience and is ideal for functional testers and developers who are new to penetration testing.

Wapiti

This open-source tool is web-based and is used for scanning web application web pages, searching for forms and scripts where data can be inserted. Wapiti is based on Python and can spot File handling errors, XSS, Database, Command execution detection, LDAP, and CRLF injections.

Webscarab

This is a framework with several plugins, written completely in Java, for examining the applications that connect via HTTP/HTTPS protocols. This tool is mainly designed for developers who can generally write code themselves.

Web Security

This is an open-source tool to automatically recognize web application vulnerabilities by utilizing fuzzing technologies and advanced discovery. It can create simple and easy reports once ran. The tool is multilingual.

The system necessities for the tools mentioned above are demonstrated in the table below:

Table Error! No text of specified style in document.-3. System necessities for the security testing tools

Tools	Requirements
BeEF	Linux, Apple Mac OS X, and Microsoft Windows
Brakeman	Rails 3
CROSS	130 protocol interfaces and formats
BFBTester – Brute Force Binary Tester	POSIX, BSD, FreeBSD, OpenBSD, Linux
Gendarme	.NET (Mono or MS runtime)
Ettercap	
Metasploit	Win32 / UNIX
Flawfinder	Python 1.5 or greater
Nmap	Linux, Windows, and Mac OS X.
Knock Subdomain Scan	Linux, Windows and MAC OS X with Python version 2.x
Oedipus	OS Independent
Nessus	Linux, Solaris, Mac, Windows
Paros	Cross-platform, Java JRE/JDK 1.4.2 or above

Nikto	Windows/UNIX
Zed Attack Proxy	Windows, Linux, Mac OS
nsiqcppstyle	Platform Independent
Skipfish	Linux, FreeBSD, macOS X, and Windows
Social Engineer Toolkit	Linux, Apple Mac OS X, and Microsoft Windows
Wapiti	Python
Vega	Java, Linux, Windows.
Web security	Unix, Linux, and Windows
WebScarab	OS Independent
Wireshark	Unix, Linux, and Windows

Chapter Seven

Web Application Security

Introduction

Varying business environments fuel progresses in web development technologies. Presently, web applications have become predominant in corporate, Government, and public services. The fundamental benefit of web applications is lies in their convenient and efficient use. However, there is a multitude of cyber-threats which can substantially damage the cyberinfrastructure of an organization. Therefore, it is essential to develop strategies to combat ever-increasing cyber-threats.

During the past three decades, the organizations have mainly relied on traditional security measures concerning the cyber-network to safeguard their critical infrastructures. However, conventional network security technologies and measures are not sufficient to protect web applications from wide-ranging cyber-threats. This is because cyber-attacks, nowadays, are precisely targeting cybersecurity flaws present in the design of various web applications. There is a need to implement novel security measures (both administrative and technological) along with the development of new web applications.

It is indispensable to comprehend the common vulnerabilities of web applications to combat the dangers linked to these application services. This chapter briefly discusses some of the precarious vulnerabilities of web applications and potential methods to deal with these vulnerabilities. Last two sections of this chapter focus on the guidelines for web application end-users to surf the Internet securely.

Web application security essentially deals with the practices of shielding online services and websites against various cybersecurity attacks that exploit susceptibilities in the code of an application. Web application attacks are usually directed towards database administration tools (i.e., PHP My Admin), SaaS applications, and content management systems (i.e., WordPress). Web applications are considered top-priority targets for attackers due to the following reasons:

i. The characteristic complexity in the web application's source code, which enhances the probability of adverse code manipulation and unattended vulnerabilities.

ii. High value compensations which includes sensitive personal data retrieved from successful manipulation of source code.

iii. Convenient execution due to possibility of automating the attacks, which can be launched extensively against millions of targets at one time.

Most organizations are faced with the danger of being attacked due to insufficient web application security. Among many other concerns, this can lead to information theft, revoked licenses, legal proceedings, and damaged client relationships.

Growing Technologies and Cyber-Threats

Rapid developments in web applications and mobile application have resulted in a competitive environment where everyone is trying to develop more products than others. This rat race has resulted in an industry with more number of products instead of quality products which fulfill the essential security requirements. The attackers can easily manipulate web applications due to the presence of security flaws.

Most of these threats are originated from session-less protocols, complexity of web technologies, network-layer insecurity, and non-trusted access points. The application developer does not completely control the client software in web applications. Therefore, the input provided by a client with a running software is not entirely administered directly. An invader can counterfeit an identity to appear like a genuine client and generate fraudulent cookies and messages. Additionally, HTTP is considered a session-less protocol that is vulnerable to injection attacks. HTTP messages can be conveniently be modified, sniffed and spoofed.

The organizations must be vigilant enough to comprehend the gravity of threats to implement suitable defensive mechanisms appropriately. Supplementary security controls (including both administrative and technical) are also required to fortify the defense of critical infrastructures during the functioning of web applications.

Administrative Controls

Some recommended administrative controls assist in reinforcement of the web application security and protect the data controlled by such applications. Key administrative controls are illustrated below:

i   It is essential to publish important guidelines to offer information regarding the development and upkeep of web applications and websites. For instance, the government of Hong Kong has published a sequence of guidelines regarding the distribution of information via government websites.

ii   There should be proper guidelines for development and coding practices used in web applications. Web application development groups should secure coding practices to develop web applications. These practices must be designed to fight security vulnerabilities in web application.

iii   The collection and management of sensitive information and user data must be carried out according to the regulations.

iv   Quality assurance and security plans must be devised, followed by the adoption of quality assurance approaches including penetration testing, code review, user acceptance test, etc.

v   A comprehensive Information Technology security audit must be performed prior to the final launch of all web applications.

Web Application Security Guidelines

To enhance the web application's security, an open-access community known as Open Web Application Security Project (i.e., OWASP) has been founded to harmonize global efforts targeted at decreasing the dangers related to web application.

A multitude of mega enterprises, as well as government organizations, has dedicated a reasonable amount of resources for the development of policies, strategies and guidelines intended for handling the threats to web applications due to their open-accessibility. Some of the world's major organizations have established checklists for assessing the overall security of the web application before its final launch. This practice ensures a minimum level of protection for a web application. For instance, the US Defense Department has established its own dedicated Application for this Security Checklist.

On the other hand, the Office of the OGCIO in Hong Kong has published a series of security guidelines and policy documents to provide the references of different government organizations. These documents are conveniently accessible at the website of OGCIO

Web Application Vulnerabilities

The OWASP is a global community dealing with web application security. OWASP makes the security of a web application "visible" to the people and enterprises so that they can make cognizant decisions about the security risks in a web application. OWASP has a consolidated list of the critical security flaws in web applications which can be accessed at:

https://www.owasp.org/index.php/Category:OWASP_Top_Ten_Project

Some of the common security flaws are illustrated in the following text. All the application developers need to be cognizant of these security flaws so that they can develop web applications with enhanced security.

Cross-Site Scripting (XSS)

Cross-site scripting allows the script execution in the browser of the victim that can lead to the hijacking of the user sessions. This flaw can be induced by inappropriate authentication if the information supplied by the user. In this case, the application takes the input data and transfers it to the web browser, unencrypted, and unvalidated.

Injection Flaws

The prospective danger of the Injection Flaw is the ability of an attacker to trick the web application into performing unintentional commands, ultimately resulting in altering system information. Injection flaws, in particular, SQL injection, are commonly found in web applications. Injection flaw takes place when the user-supplied input is transferred as component of the query or command to the interpreter.

Malicious File Execution

This kind of threat attacks the code of a file, and the phenomenon is known as remote file inclusion (RFI). This attack on the code can allow the intruders to incorporate hostile data and code into the existing code, ultimately resulting in dangerous attacks, e.g., compromising the entire server. Attacks powered by malicious file execution can adversely affect XML, PHP and similar frameworks that receive files or filenames from users.

Direct Object Insecure Reference

The prospective danger in case of direct object insecure reference entails the power of an attacker to exploit the references to make other objects accessible without authentication. An Insecure direct object reference takes place when a reference is exposed to the internal execution object, for example, a file, database record, directory, as a form or URL parameter, by the developer.

Cross-Site Request Forgery (i.e., CSRF)

This kind of threat attacks the browser of the logged-on victim. The browser is modified to send pre-authenticated requests to a risk-susceptible web application, which results in the execution of hostile actions by the browser. CSRF attack can be extremely powerful even more than the web application under attack.

Improper Error Handling and Information Leakage

The potential danger from this kind of flaw is the ability of the attacker to steal sensitive information. Comprehensive attacks can also lead to a chain of attacks on various applications. Vulnerable applications can inadvertently disclose their configuration data and internal workings. Moreover, there is also a chance of privacy violations through a range of application issues.

Session Management and Broken Authentication

This kind of flaw may be caused when account credentials and session tokens are not protected properly. Attackers can exploit this flaw to assume the user's identity by compromising keys, passwords, and authentication tokens.

Insecure Cryptographic Storage

Flaws like this arise because of improper cryptographic functions of web applications to protect credentials and data. Attackers use this kind of flaw to exploit the sensitive data of the victims for carrying out identity theft, credit card fraud, etc.

Insecure Communications

When sensitive data is leaked over an infrastructure of network communication, it can result in insecure communications. This kind of flaw is mainly caused by the inability of a web application and network security protocols to encrypt the network traffic.

Failure to Restrict URL Access

This flaw is instigated by web applications that only safeguard sensitive functionality by preventing the demonstration of URLs or links to unauthorized users. However, the attackers can hijack the information by directly accessing the URLs.

Web Application Security Guidelines

As previously stated in this chapter, advanced security hazards come with the advantages of deploying web applications. Several security controls must be implemented during the complete course of the development lifespan of the project to deal with these risks in an effective manner. In the following section, we will go through the lifespan phase by phase for understanding at what point in the lifespan a particular security control is recommended. Furthermore, the main security concerns requiring special attention have been mentioned, as well.

The Requirement Stage

At this stage, it is the responsibility of the application development team to collect all the systems as well as security data from different parties taking part in the project. These system requirements should specify specifications needed by the development team, providing an overview of the main purpose of the application, as well as the do's and don't of the application. With the help of this data, the development team will be able to define vital security controls for the application.

Moreover, certain security mechanisms are needed to be developed into the application to comply with requirements or regulations. For instance, the PCI DSS (Payment Card Industry Data Security Standard) emphases on establishing such controls which reduces the presence of security susceptibilities both in software and systems.

Additionally, it postulates requirements for secure software development as well as protection from attacks. We can say that establishing system and user security requirements accurately is imperative in driving the design, development, and finally, during testing stages, since this will upturn the general security of the web application and guarantee greater user contentment with the end result.

The Design Stage

The design stage comprises designing the application according to the specifications defined in the first stage; moreover, the design stage involves performing threat modeling, defining secure coding standards, and developing security architecture for the application.

Definition of Secure Coding Standards

Secure coding standards specifies the guidelines instructing the developers on how to write the code for the web application; it further should specify guidelines and instructions for developing secure code and identifying high-risk areas, error handling, and data input. Different organizations have recommended numerous secure coding practices such as CERT and OWASP. The OGCIO, in their IT Security Guidelines, have mentioned a set of common secure coding practices:

1. Endorse all input parameters for inhibiting attacks like cross-site scripting attacks and SQL injection:

   A centralized module should be developed by the programmers to carry out validation of the input parameter and checking of each input parameter against a particular format which specifies exactly what types of input will be permitted. It is important to filter special characters like "$%^~!#&*[]\r\n<>" coming from the input, or else should be substituted with an escape sequence. Client-side scripts must not be trusted to carry out the essential validation checks.

   The application must only take in data comprising a strictly restricted and anticipated set of characters. If a number is anticipated, then the application should only accept digits. If a word is expected, then only letters should be permitted. Input data must also be endorsed for the proper format. If the application expects an email address, then only numbers, letters, the "at" (@) symbol, dots, and dashes in the proper arrangement should be allowed. The application can also include enforcing maximum and minimum length restrictions on all incoming traffic. This method can be used for session credentials, account numbers, usernames, and so on. All these practices limit the magnitude of potential entry points for incoming attacks.

2. Sanitized application response

For sanitization, a centralized module must be developed. All return codes, output, as well as error codes from calls (for instance, calls to the backend database) must be tested to make sure that the normal processing is actually occurring. For instance, excessive internal system information like internal hostnames, directory structures, internal IP addresses, verbose error messages produced by internal server errors throughout a response must not be revealed on the client-side.

3. HTTP trust issues

Programmers must not depend or trust on HTTP REFERER headers, cookies, or form fields for making security decisions since attackers can spoof this kind of data. Unless and until some strong cryptographic methods are used for verifying the integrity of HTTP headers, we should not trust such parameters approaching from a client browser. Furthermore, it must not be assumed that the user cannot alter hidden parameters since attackers can easily manipulate hidden parameters.

4. Sensitive session values should be kept on the server to avoid client-side modification

Any sensitive data should not be put in any client browser cookies. In case sensitive data has to be saved in a client browser, resilient cryptographic methods must be implemented to protect the integrity and confidentiality of the data.

5. Encrypt pages which contain any sensitive data and prevent caching

During transmission, proper algorithms and keys like TLS and SSL should be used to encrypt pages that contain sensitive data. Additionally, make use of ActiveX or signed Java applets for obtaining and displaying sensitive data, as well as set the suitable HTTP header attributes for preventing caching by proxy or through the browser, of a particular page given that page contain sensitive data.

6. Session management

A session ID has to be complicated, long, and comprise of random, unpredictable numbers. Furthermore, it must be regularly changed during a session to cut short the time duration of validation of a session ID. Besides, a session ID must not be saved in a URL, hidden HTML fields, persistent cookies, or else HTTP headers.

Programmers should contemplate storing session IDs in session cookies of a client's browser. Session IDs can be guarded against sniffing through attackers by using TLS or SSL. One more precaution is to implement a logout function as well as an idle session timeout for the application. At the time of logging out or timing-out during an idle session, if possible, the client-side cookies should be cleared; moreover, the server-side session state for that browser as well as connections to backend servers must also be cleaned up.

7. Access restriction

It should be made sure that the end-user account has certain rights to access only those functions which are authorized to access, limiting access to the backend database. At the time an application makes system calls for accessing specific programs, no calls should be made to authentic file names and directory paths. If hackers have access to the source code, they might be able to expose system-level information.

8. A centralized module should be built for application auditing and reporting.

9. The most suitable type of authentication method must be used for the job of identifying and authenticating incoming user requests.

Performing Threat Modeling

To build a secure application, a complete understanding of the threats against that particular application is needed. A threat modeling procedure aids in the identification of susceptibilities, threats, attacks, and countermeasures in the context of that particular application scenario. Following steps can be adopted to accomplish threat modeling:

Step 1: Recognize the main security objectives.

Step 2: Build an overview of the application by listing the significant features of that application.

Step 3: Deconstruct the application for identifying the characteristics and modules which have a security effect, and which must be evaluated.

Step 4: Identify all security threats

Step 5: Identify all security susceptibilities.

Designing of Security Architecture for Web Application

The architecture of a characteristic web application comprises three tiers, separating the internal application server as well as database server from externally-facing web server. By implementing such a tier-based architecture, even if an invader gets through an externally-facing web server, they still have to discover means for acquiring access and attacking the internal network. This is the norm of defense-in-depth protection, making it a practical approach to information security. The basic concept continually centers on the idea of the application of multiple layers of security for the protection of significant assets. Multiple security layers include validation of input, the configuration of the server, proxies, database layer abstraction, web application firewalls, OS hardening, data encryption, and so on.

The Development Stage

The development stage is the most significant in terms of alleviating security concerns within the code. Observation of secure coding standards definitely aids in improving security and decreasing the number of common mistakes that outcome in security breaches. Moreover, carrying out security risk assessments throughout the development stage also aids in identifying the security controls needed.

The Testing and Quality Assurance Stage

The necessity for comprehensive testing is vital prior to the launching of any application for production. Besides user acceptance tests, there are several other tests such as stress tests, system tests, unit tests, and regression tests, which are beneficial for validation of performance and accurateness of system functionalities. These tests further increase the security and reliability of the systems being developed. Below mentioned are examples of some of such tests.

Web Application Unit Testing

Web application unit testing is a significant portion of the development stage and is designed for identifying the weaknesses in a web application. Unit testing comprises the testing of individual modules to make sure that all internal operations of that module or program are performing as per the specifications. Unit testing must contain tests for common security concerns like buffer overflows and is particularly imperative if the module or program is being integrated into a "build" with other modules. In case no unit tests are performed, it gets extremely difficult to execute an automatic security testing procedure in the course of the development stage.

Several tools are available which can help in finding and eliminating web application susceptibilities; however, it must be noted that such tools can only cover a small portion of the testing required for a successful application security program. To rely solely on tools instead of focusing on refining the software development life cycle results in an incorrect sense of security, since automated scanning tools can only identify and uncover limited types of vulnerabilities.

Code Review

A peer review method, commenced by detail examination of source code can aid in identifying security flaws, and thus make sure observance of standards of security development, as well as consistency with the complete design of the program. Generally, system administrators, development managers, as well as database administrators, would be present for examining the mechanisms of the source code of the application. All these parties can suggest and recommend improvements. Moreover, a detail examination of the source code helps in identifying secure or hidden content, like passwords and keys, as well as can help in evaluation of the sufficiency of applied protective measures.

Numerous automated code scanning tools can be found in the market, which might help to share some burden of the code-walkthrough. However, in the case of web application scanning tools, such tools might only be capable of identifying common errors and not more complicated security problems. Hence, such tools must not be considered an alternative to human analysis.

The Pre-Production Stage

Prior to the launch of production as well as before any significant system changes, an IT security audit should be carried out. Each susceptibility fix needs updates to custom code; moreover, each repair needs a code push which sometimes can introduce a new system vulnerability. Hence, it is important to constantly assess the effect of each repair to maintain secure applications.

The Support and Maintenance Stage

Cybersecurity is a constant process. We can find security problems in a web application even after its release in the market. Therefore, it is indispensable to develop mechanisms for threat detection and application protection to ensure the smooth and secure running of the application. Some of the essential security strategies are demonstrated in following sub-headings.

Application Log Review

The log review is important in order to detect the anomalies in an application accurately. Various web servers are integrated with comprehensive logs to track the web requests directed towards a web application. It is quite possible to investigate the vulnerability of a web application by studying the access log of the web application and reviewing the requests directed towards the web application. This practice can demonstrate the true picture of web application safety. For instance, the web application might be under attack if any anomaly is observed in the URLs.

Additionally, the execution of audit trails for the application can also be requested by the web application owners. In short, all end-users and application owners need to review exception reports, anomalous transactions, and undefined requests.

Version Control

The application integrity must be upheld using suitable cybersecurity controls, including version control mechanisms, environments separation for application development, live operation, acceptance testing, and system testing. It is also essential to keep the development and production environments synchronized. To implement the strategy mentioned above, the companies must set some ground rules. For instance, the staff of the application development department must not be authorized to access production data without a valid reason.

Firewalls for Web Applications

Most of the standard firewall versions can assist in restriction or permission of network access to designated network ports that are approved by the companies. Application proxy firewall is also in operation for most of the web applications, but they cannot comprehend the specific data linked to all web applications which are being operated by a particular organization. The Web Application Security Consortium defined the web application firewall (i.e., WAF) as: *"an intermediary device, sitting between a web-client and a web server, analyzing OSI Layer7 messages for violations in the programmed security policy"*.

Installation of firewalls for web applications are usually carried out adjacent to the webserver. Similar to standard firewall versions, these web firewalls (either in hardware or software form) are designed to protect the server from cyber-attacks. Following are two key methods of severing protection:

i.   Abnormal/anomalous behavior based: This approach deals with the identification of attacks by the WAF by sensing anomalous traffic behavior.

ii. Signature-based: This approach mainly focuses on attack identification by the WAF by inspecting web requests against a particular *"attack signature"* file.

Checklist for Acceptance of a Web Application

After web application acceptance, a security assessment must be carried out to guarantee thorough compliance with project cybersecurity prerequisites or organizational policy by evaluating the source code and the web application. This evaluation is a necessary tool for all projects related to a web application that is likely to be outsourced to independent development centers. It is also essential to integrate the security control test cases (needed in the initiation phase of the project) with the User Acceptance Test.

Security considerations must be prioritized above all other requirements in the initiation phase of a project. Security necessities and expectations — particularly audit trail requirements, need for authentication mechanisms and input validation demands— should be conversed with development houses.

The following sections illustrate the examples of potential arenas that must be included for examination in web application security evaluation.

Identification and Authorization

Following questions must be asked to resolve identification and authorization issues:

i.   How is authentication of processes, and are users performed?

ii. Is the implementation of the authorization process in agreement with stipulations and security policies of the company?

iii. If passwords are used for authentication, what are the handling and storage procedures for the user passwords?

iv. Are the password storage and handling mechanisms in agreement with the security rules and policies of the organization?

v. Is there any embedded hard-coded key or password in the source of a program?

vi. Is authentication required by the application for all sessions?

Data Protection

i. What is the mechanism of data protection?

ii. Does the mechanism of data protection comply with the organizational security policy?

iii. What is the state of the protected data? Is it all at rest or in transit?

iv. Is encryption being implemented during data handling? Does the data encryption and handling show compliance with organizational security policies?

Logging

i. What type of audit trail logging mechanism is being implemented?

ii. Do the audit trail logging mechanisms comply with organizational specifications?

iii. Is there any vulnerability of audit records to unauthenticated modification, deletion, or disclosure?

Error Handling

    i. What is the handling mechanism for error messages?

    ii. Are there any chances of a data breach or data leak that could be exploited in a consequent cyber-attack?

    iii. Can the application failure lead to the vulnerability of the whole system?

Operation

    i. Has the removal of all IDs (including built-in IDs, default IDs and testing IDs) been carried out before the final launch of the web application?

    ii. Is there a proper implementation of least privilege principles and segregation of duties?

    iii. Are there fully defined procedures for system administration, disaster recovery, change management, and backup?

It is pertinent to note here that the above-discussed list is not exhaustive. The users and application developers can add or subtract the checklist items according to the requirements of a particular web application.

Additionally, in the case of outsourced projects, there must be an established mechanism for security management for all the web applications to safeguard the information as well as to alleviate the cybersecurity dangers linked to outsourced projects.

Guidelines for Web Protection during Internet Surfing

End-users of a web application need to take some essential steps to safeguard themselves from cyber threats. Nowadays, it is very common to install applications after agreeing to their terms and conditions. Most of these web applications make their users agree that the service provider of the web application will not be responsible for any damage or loss that may take place because of cybersecurity breaches. The following strategies can be implemented by the end-users to safeguard web applications against potential cyber-attacks.

1. Do not use a public computer to log in to any important web application.

2. Do not allow the cache of your password and username in a workstation.

3. Ensure logging-off after the session ends.

4. Use variable user-logins and passcodes for different services and web applications.

5. Make sure to change the passwords of web applications regularly.

6. Activate the feature of using a one-time password if the applications support it.

7. Instantly report all anomalous behaviors of the web application to your service provider.

8. Make sure to patch and update the operating system modules, e.g., Internet Explorer, Mozilla Firefox, Google Chrome, Tor Browser, etc.

9. Install the latest version of antivirus and firewall. The installed anti-virus software must be powerful enough to detect dangerous viruses, e.g., malware, Trojan, etc.

10. Avoid downloading software and their plug-ins from unauthentic sources.

Guidelines for Eliminating Security Vulnerabilities in a Code

The OWASP (Open.Web.Application.Security.Project) explored the ten top-most serious cybersecurity vulnerabilities existing in most of the web applications. The OWASP team focuses on both the identification and elimination of critical vulnerabilities from the code of web application. The OWASP website provides the following recommendations to combat cyber-attacks on web applications.

1. A standard validation mechanism must be used to ensure the validation of all input data.

2. Strong encoding of the output must be ensured.

3. The output encoding must be specified (e.g., UTF 8 or ISO 8859-1).

4. Use of straightforward escaping functions must be avoided.

5. The use of "blacklist" validations for detecting XSS must be prohibited in input validation and output encoding.

6. Comprehensive error messages must be avoided.

7. Canonicalization errors must be monitored.

8. Powerfully typed query APIs with designated parameters must be used.

9. Least privilege must be enforced.

10. Care must be shown while dealing with stored procedures.

11. Use of interfaces with dynamic queries must not be used.

12. The indirect reference map should be used for objects.

13. Firewall rules must be added to inhibit web servers from establishing new connections to internal systems and external websites.

14. Constant checking of user-supplied filenames or files must be ensured.

15. Exposure of your personal object references must be avoided to the maximum possible extent.

16. The use of GET requests for URLs must be avoided for the protection of sensitive data during value transactions.

17. Explicit taint inspection mechanisms should be used.

18. Validation of any personal object references must be performed comprehensively using the "accept known good" technique.

19. Implementation of "chroot jail" can be a good option for web application security.

20. Authorization for all referenced objects must be verified.

21. Every URL and form must be inserted with custom random tokens.

22. Re-authentication or transaction signing must be used for sensitive data transactions.

Chapter Eight

Cybersecurity Measures

Introduction

According to an estimate, the Internet uses more than 3.3 billion residents, and around 9.9 billion mobile phones, computers, and other devices from all over the world are connected with the Internet. This quantity is continually growing, resulting in increasing demands of security measures. The most widespread security concern on the Internet is viruses that attack daily. Cybercriminals make use of viruses to fall into the computer system. It is indispensable to select a suitable operating system that is reliable, stable, as well as resistant to most damaging programs. Another important task is to install suitable antivirus programs that can detect and terminate such programs. Some common good practices include creating backups of all significant data, taking extreme precautions while downloading files from the Internet as well as while opening any email account, and updating the programs etc. A big number of security issues to the system of huge networks remain undetected for months and the viruses remain unnoticed in the system. Therefore, special focus needs to be paid for protecting the undetected viruses and undisclosed attacks. It is indispensable to employ such early detection algorithms, and monitoring systems that can provide warning and potential instinctive response to system failures. In this chapter, we have outlined some basic measures which must be implemented for increasing the security level of computer and network systems.

Maintaining Correct Catalogue of Control Systems and Eliminating Equipment Exposure to Outside Networks

Any machine on the control network should never be allowed to talk directly to a machine on the Internet or on the business network. Even if industrial control systems of any organization is not directly connected to the Internet, still, a connection subsists if such systems are linked with a part of the network – for instance, the corporate side – which can have a communication channel to outside resources (Internet).

Despite organizations not realizing the existence of any such connection, an insistent cyber threat performer can discover such ways and use them for exploiting industrial control systems. Hence, organizations should carry out detailed assessments of their systems, as well as their corporate enterprise segments for determining the existence of such pathways.

Implementing Firewalls and Network Segmentation

Network segmentation involves classification and categorization of data, IT assets, and personnel into particular groups, and then limiting access to these groups. Placement of resources into different network areas helps to avoid the exploitation of the entire system since the security compromise of one sector won't be translating into the whole system. With the increase in the use of "Internet of Things," numerous formerly non-Internet connected devices, for instance, video cameras, are now connected to systems and the internet making the significance of segmenting networks more than ever.

We can limit access to network areas by completely isolating them from one another, which is ideal in the circumstances of industrial control systems, or through implementing firewalls. A firewall is any hardware device or any software program which filters both the inbound as well as outbound traffic among various network parts or a network and the Internet. Thus, a firewall can be implemented for filtering incoming and outgoing information in case of connections facing the Internet. By decreasing the number of entry paths into networks and by executing security protocols on the existing paths, threats are not likely to enter and gain access to the system.

Using Secure Remote Access Methods

The facility of remote connection to any network has greatly facilitated end users. However, it is advisable to use a secure access method like a Virtual Private Network (VPN), in case of remote access is needed. A Virtual Private Network is an encrypted data channel for both sending and securely receiving data through public IT infrastructure (for example, the Internet). Users can remotely access internal resources such as printers, files, websites, or databases through a VPN just like a direct connection to the network. It is even possible to further harden this remote access by decreasing the number of IP addresses accessing it. However, it must be noted that a VPN is simply as secure as the devices linked to it. An infected computer can introduce susceptibilities into the network, resulting in additional infections and contradicting the security of the VPN.

Establishing Role-Based Access Controls

Role-based access control, based on job function, either grants or rejects access to network resources, thereby limiting the accessibility of users or attackers to files or parts of the system that they shouldn't access. For instance, the operators of SCADA system probably do not require access to specific administrative files. Hence, permissions should be defined based on the level of access each job requires to carry out its duties, and standard operating procedures should be implemented for removing network access of ex-employees. Moreover, through restraining employee permissions via role-based access controls, we can help in identifying network intrusions or any doubtful activities during an audit.

Monitoring network traffic further permits organizations to decide if a worker is engaged in unauthorized actions or if there is an outsider present is in the system, thus providing a chance to intervene prior to the manifestation of problems.

Using Strong Passwords and Considering Methods of Alternate Access Controls

Strong passwords must be used for keeping information and systems secure. Moreover, there should be different passwords for different accounts. Attackers can employ different software tools to try an unauthorized login called "brute force attack." There should be at least eight characters in a password. However, longer passwords are stronger, as there are a greater number of characters that need to be guessed.

Additionally, both uppercase and lowercase letters as well as special characters, and numerals should be included. Upon installing any new software, such as for control system devices and administrator accounts, all default passwords must be changed and regularly updated afterward. We can also implement other password security practices, like an account lock-out which activates after numerous attempts of incorrect passwords. Organizations might also take into account demanding multi-factor authentication, involving users to verify their identities through codes sent to devices on which they are formally registered – every time they try to sign-in.

Maintaining Vulnerability Awareness and Implementing Essential Updates and Patches

Most retailers work carefully for the development of patches to identify vulnerabilities. Nonetheless, even after the release of patches and updates, numerous systems remain vulnerable for the reason that organizations are either not aware of or opt to not implement these fixes. According to a Data Breach Investigations Report of 2016, Verizon found that in the majority of industries, around three-quarters of breach incidents have been covered only through three patterns, which were denial of service, cyber espionage, and crimeware. As per its recommendations, to detect breaches and create defenses, it is imperative to understand the building blocks of an attack (for example, a kill chain). Effective patching can also help in stopping a large share of attacks.

According to Cisco's 2016 Annual Security Report, security professionals should reconsider their defense tactics since cybercriminals have sophisticated their infrastructures for carrying out attacks in a more effective manner. Thus, it is important to implement a system of monitoring and executing system patches and updates to defend one's organization against such devious attacks.

Organizations should also deliberate on setting such software and systems which can auto-update to evade missing serious updates. Such updates are intended to fix identified vulnerabilities and are therefore encouraged for any type of Internet-connected device.

Implementing Cybersecurity Training Program for Employees

Cybersecurity for critical infrastructure areas that drive industrial control systems is particularly important since these systems are progressively being targeted. If workers aren't involved in cybersecurity, it can not only result in non-detection of vulnerabilities and threats; moreover, the workers themselves can become channels of execution of attacks. For that reason, workers should be given initial as well as periodic cybersecurity training to help maintain the security of the business/ organization.

Although cybersecurity is an extensive field, there are specific topics which must be stressed for creating general awareness. An example of such a topic is social engineering, which remains a popular choice for cyber attackers to target innocent employees. Social engineering methods involve phishing, phone calls, or any other types of personal interactions through which wicked performers try to tempt employees into providing sensitive corporate or personal data like account passwords or details about infrastructure. Unwelcomed phone calls, emails, as well as other correspondence from unknown sources, should be observed with more caution.

Another popular method of attack is spear-phishing, in which the vulnerabilities are the workers who are comprised of social engineering. According to a survey, in 2015, the water and dams sectors summed up 31 such incidents in total.

Training must also include the significance of adopting smart Internet browsing practices. By visiting distrustful websites, users might get exposed to the infection through malware embedded on the website. It is even possible that genuine websites and files on them can be compromised. Cyber attackers' uses a variation of this sort of tactic known as a "watering-hole" attack, for targeting such workers of a company about which they know will visit the malicious website. Hence, care should be taken no matter where a worker traverses and the materials which are downloaded from the internet.

Involving Executives in Cybersecurity

Insignificant attention is paid to Cybersecurity in most of the companies. Executives do not play any role in controlling the aspects of cybersecurity until some mishaps happen. Presently, most of the organizations are enhancing cybersecurity to the level of the executives by incorporating the position of CISO (Chief Information Security Officer). 'Securing the C-Suite' is an IBM's paper which surveyed around 700 executives globally to assess the understanding of executives about cyber threats. The survey results showed that there were four signs which indicate the unpreparedness of the organizations against cybersecurity threats. These threats include the misidentification of threats, non-inclusion of C-Suite members in Cybersecurity plans, reluctance in sharing cybersecurity threats with external companies, and the lack of a CISO.

Conclusion

This book offers a comprehensive overview of the essential components and methods of cybersecurity. The accomplishment of an effective Cybersecurity approach in an organization is a combined responsibility of people, processes, technology, computers, and networks of an organization. It is essential to integrate all the components of an organization into a single cybersecurity agenda. If all components of an organization complement each other in all aspects of cybersecurity, it is quite possible to stand against the threatening cyber-attacks.

References

Abomhara, Mohamed. "Cybersecurity and the internet of things: vulnerabilities, threats, intruders and attacks." *Journal of Cybersecurity and Mobility* 4, no. 1 (2015): 65-88.

Adam, Alison. "Cyberstalking and Internet pornography: Gender and the gaze." *Ethics and Information Technology* 4, no. 2 (2002): 133-142.

Adams, Paul C., and Barney Warf. "Introduction: Cyberspace and geographical space." *Geographical Review* (1997): 139-145.

Adams, Terrence. "AI-powered social bots." *arXiv preprint arXiv:1706.05143* (2017).

Aikat, Debashis. "Adventure in cyberspace: Exploring the information content of the World Wide Web pages on the Internet." (1996).

Albert, Réka, Hawoong Jeong, and Albert-László Barabási. "Internet: Diameter of the world-wide web." *nature* 401, no. 6749 (1999): 130.

Alexy, Eileen M., Ann W. Burgess, Timothy Baker, and Shirley A. Smoyak. "Perceptions of cyberstalking among college students." *Brief Treatment & Crisis Intervention* 5, no. 3 (2005).

Allen, Julia H., Sean Barnum, Robert J. Ellison, Gary McGraw, and Nancy R. Mead. *Software security engineering*. Pearson India, 2008.

Alomari, Esraa, Selvakumar Manickam, B. B. Gupta, Shankar Karuppayah, and Rafeef Alfaris. "Botnet-based distributed denial of service (DDoS) attacks on web servers: classification and art." *arXiv preprint arXiv:1208.0403* (2012).

Andrew S. Tanenbaum. *Computer networks*. Prentice Hall Professional, 2003.

Antón, Annie I., Julia Brande Earp, and Angela Reese. "Analyzing website privacy requirements using a privacy goal taxonomy." In *Proceedings IEEE Joint International Conference on Requirements Engineering*, pp. 23-31. IEEE, 2002.

Aradau, Claudia. "Security that matters: Critical infrastructure and objects of protection." *Security dialogue* 41, no. 5 (2010): 491-514.

Armstrong, Helen L., and Patrick J. Forde. "Internet anonymity practices in computer crime." *Information management & computer security* 11, no. 5 (2003): 209-215.

Babar, Sachin, Parikshit Mahalle, Antonietta Stango, Neeli Prasad, and Ramjee Prasad. "Proposed security model and threat taxonomy for the Internet of Things (IoT)." In *International Conference on Network Security and Applications*, pp. 420-429. Springer, Berlin, Heidelberg, 2010.

Barron, D. A. "Subscriber trunk dialing. The scheme for full automation of the telephone service in the United Kingdom." *Proceedings of the IEE-Part B: Electronic and Communication Engineering* 106, no. 28 (1959): 341-360.

Bass, Tim, Alfredo Freyre, David Gruber, and Glenn Watt. "E-mail bombs and countermeasures: cyber attacks on availability and brand integrity." *IEEE Network* 12, no. 2 (1998): 10-17.

Bergholz, André, Jan De Beer, Sebastian Glahn, Marie-Francine Moens, Gerhard Paaß, and Siehyun Strobel. "New filtering approaches for phishing email." *Journal of computer security* 18, no. 1 (2010): 7-35.

Berners-Lee, Tim, Dimitri Dimitroyannis, A. John Mallinckrodt, and Susan McKay. "World Wide Web." *Computers in Physics* 8, no. 3 (1994): 298-299.

Beyda, William J. *Data communications: From basics to broadband.* Prentice Hall PTR, 1999.

Bhasin, Madan. "Mitigating cyber threats to banking industry." *The Chartered Accountant* 50, no. 10 (2007): 1618-1624.

Biju, Jibi Mariam, Neethu Gopal, and Anju J. Prakash. "CYBER ATTACKS AND ITS DIFFERENT TYPES." (2019).

Bologna, Sandro, and Roberto Setola. "The need to improve local self-awareness in CIP/CIIP." In *First IEEE International Workshop on Critical Infrastructure Protection (IWCIP'05),* pp. 6-pp. IEEE, 2005.

Braud, Luke A., Baruch Goldwasser, and Evan M. Goldberg. "Facilitating data manipulation in a browser-based user interface of an enterprise business application." U.S. Patent 7,685,515, issued March 23, 2010.

Bunker, V. Nelson Waldo, David Laizerovich, Eva Elizabeth Bunker, and Joey Don Van Schuyver. "Network security testing." U.S. Patent 7,325,252, issued January 29, 2008.

Burden, Kit, and Creole Palmer. "Internet crime: Cyber Crime—A new breed of criminal?." *Computer Law & Security Review* 19, no. 3 (2003): 222-227.

Byres, Eric, P. Eng, and I. S. A. Fellow. "Using ANSI/ISA-99 standards to improve control system security." *White paper, Tofino Security* (2012).

Caldwell, Tracey. "Ethical hackers: putting on the white hat." *Network Security* 2011, no. 7 (2011): 10-13.

Cerezo, Ana I., Javier Lopez, and Ahmed Patel. "International cooperation to fight transnational cybercrime." In *Second international workshop on digital forensics and incident analysis (WDFIA 2007)*, pp. 13-27. IEEE, 2007.

Chaisiri, Sivadon, Ryan KL Ko, and Dusit Niyato. "A joint optimization approach to security-as-a-service allocation and cyber insurance management." In *2015 IEEE Trustcom/bigdatase/ispa*, vol. 1, pp. 426-433. IEEE, 2015.

Chakrabarti, Anirban, and G. Manimaran. "Internet infrastructure security: A taxonomy." *IEEE network* 16, no. 6 (2002): 13-21.

Chen, Yanpei, Vern Paxson, and Randy H. Katz. "What's new about cloud computing security." *University of California, Berkeley*

Report No. UCB/EECS-2010-5 January 20, no. 2010 (2010): 2010-5.

Chen, Zesheng, and Chuanyi Ji. "An information-theoretic view of network-aware malware attacks." *IEEE Transactions on Information Forensics and Security* 4, no. 3 (2009): 530-541.

Chenette, Stephan, and Rajesh Kumar Sharma. "Cybersecurity Posture Validation Platform." U.S. Patent Application 14/818,975, filed February 11, 2016.

Cheswick, William Roberts, and Edward G. Whitten. "Firewall security method and apparatus." U.S. Patent Application 09/047,207, filed February 6, 2001.

Choi, Hyunsang, Bin B. Zhu, and Heejo Lee. "Detecting Malicious Web Links and Identifying Their Attack Types." *WebApps* 11, no. 11 (2011): 218.

Choi, Kyung-shick. "Computer crime victimization and integrated theory: An empirical assessment." *International Journal of Cyber Criminology* 2, no. 1 (2008).

Choi, MinSuk, Yair Levy, and Anat Hovav. "The role of user computer self-efficacy, cybersecurity countermeasures awareness, and cybersecurity skills influence on computer misuse." In *Proceedings of the Pre-International Conference of Information Systems (ICIS) SIGSEC–Workshop on Information Security and Privacy (WISP)*. 2013.

Choo, Kim-Kwang Raymond. "The cyber threat landscape: Challenges and future research directions." *Computers & Security* 30, no. 8 (2011): 719-731.

Chow, Stanley Taihai, Vinod Choyi, and Dmitri Vinokurov. "Caller name authentication to prevent caller identity spoofing." U.S. Patent 9,241,013, issued January 19, 2016.

Cios, Krzysztof J., Witold Pedrycz, and Roman W. Swiniarski. "Data mining and knowledge discovery." In *Data mining methods for knowledge discovery*, pp. 1-26. Springer, Boston, MA, 1998.

Citron, Danielle Keats. "Cyber civil rights." *BUL Rev.* 89 (2009): 61.

Claffy, Kimberly C., Hans-Werner Braun, and George C. Polyzos. "Tracking long-term growth of the NSFNET." *Communications of the ACM* 37, no. 8 (1994): 34-45.

Cleveland, Frances M. "Cybersecurity issues for advanced metering infrasttructure (AMI)." In *2008 IEEE Power and Energy Society General Meeting-Conversion and Delivery of Electrical Energy in the 21st Century*, pp. 1-5. IEEE, 2008.

Cohen, Fred. "Simulating cyber attacks, defences, and consequences." *Computers & Security* 18, no. 6 (1999): 479-518.

Cohen-Almagor, Raphael. "Internet history." In *Moral, Ethical, and Social Dilemmas in the Age of Technology: Theories and Practice*, pp. 19-39. IGI Global, 2013.

Conteh, Nabie Y., and Paul J. Schmick. "Cybersecurity: risks, vulnerabilities and countermeasures to prevent social engineering attacks." *International Journal of Advanced Computer Research* 6, no. 23 (2016): 31.

Conti, Gregory, and Kulsoom Abdullah. "Passive visual fingerprinting of network attack tools." In *Proceedings of the 2004 ACM workshop on Visualization and data mining for computer security*, pp. 45-54. ACM, 2004.

Cook, Allan, Helge Janicke, Leandros Maglaras, and Richard Smith. "An assessment of the application of IT security mechanisms to industrial control systems." *International Journal of Internet Technology and Secured Transactions* 7, no. 2 (2017): 144-174.

Corbin, Roberta A. "The development of the national research and education network." *Information technology and libraries* 10, no. 3 (1991): 212-20.

Cotton, Michelle, Lars Eggert, Joe Touch, Magnus Westerlund, and Stuart Cheshire. "Internet Assigned Numbers Authority (IANA) Procedures for the Management of the Service Name and Transport Protocol Port Number Registry." *RFC* 6335 (2011): 1-33.

Cruz, Tiago, Jorge Proença, Paulo Simões, Matthieu Aubigny, Moussa Ouedraogo, Antonio Graziano, and Leandros Maglaras. "A distributed IDS for industrial control systems." *International Journal of Cyber Warfare and Terrorism (IJCWT)* 4, no. 2 (2014): 1-22.

Cruz, Tiago, Luis Rosa, Jorge Proença, Leandros Maglaras, Matthieu Aubigny, Leonid Lev, Jianmin Jiang, and Paulo Simoes. "A cybersecurity detection framework for supervisory control and data acquisition systems." *IEEE Transactions on Industrial Informatics* 12, no. 6 (2016): 2236-2246.

Curphey, Mark, and Rudolph Arawo. "Web application security assessment tools." *IEEE Security & Privacy* 4, no. 4 (2006): 32-41.

Dashora, Kamini. "Cyber crime in the society: Problems and preventions." *Journal of Alternative Perspectives in the social sciences* 3, no. 1 (2011): 240-259.

Dayan, Richard A., Kimthanh D. Le, Matthew T. Mittelstedt, Palmer E. Newman, Dave L. Randall, Lisa A. Ruotolo, and JoAnna B. Yoder. "LAN station personal computer system with controlled data access for normal and unauthorized users and method." U.S. Patent 5,287,519, issued February 15, 1994.

Deng, Hongmei, Wei Li, and Dharma P. Agrawal. "Routing security in wireless ad hoc networks." *IEEE Communications magazine* 40, no. 10 (2002): 70-75.

Denning, Peter J. "The science of computing: The ARPANET after twenty years." *American Scientist* 77, no. 6 (1989): 530-534.

Deo, Vinay. "System and method for protecting unauthorized access to data contents." U.S. Patent 5,594,227, issued January 14, 1997.

DiGiorgio, Rinaldo, and Michael S. Bender. "Secure token device access to services provided by an internet service provider (ISP)." U.S. Patent 6,385,729, issued May 7, 2002.

Don, Arieh, Ofer E. Michael, Patrick Brian Riordan, Ian Wigmore, and Anestis Panidis. "Non-disruptive migration using device identity spoofing and passive/active ORS pull sessions." U.S. Patent 8,060,710, issued November 15, 2011.

Dunham, Ken. *Mobile malware attacks and defense.* Syngress, 2008.

Dusberger, Dariusz. "Image storage and reference using a URL." U.S. Patent Application 09/920,070, filed February 6, 2003.

Egevang, Kjeld, and Paul Francis. *The IP network address translator (NAT).* RFC 1631, may, 1994.

Eisenmann, Caroline. "When hackers turn to blackmail." *Harvard Business Review* 1 (2009): 39-42.

Eldar, Avigdor, Itamar Sharoni, Tsippy Mendelson, and Uri Blumenthal. "Techniques for password attack mitigation." U.S. Patent 8,132,018, issued March 6, 2012.

Enck, William, Damien Octeau, Patrick D. McDaniel, and Swarat Chaudhuri. "A study of android application security." In *USENIX security symposium*, vol. 2, p. 2. 2011.

Ericsson, Göran N. "Cybersecurity and power system communication—essential parts of a smart grid infrastructure." *IEEE Transactions on Power Delivery* 25, no. 3 (2010): 1501-1507.

Evans, Mark, Leandros A. Maglaras, Ying He, and Helge Janicke. "Human behaviour as an aspect of cybersecurity assurance." *Security and Communication Networks* 9, no. 17 (2016): 4667-4679.

Fabro, Mark. *Control systems cybersecurity: Defense-in-depth strategies.* No. INL/CON-07-12804. Idaho National Laboratory (INL), 2007.

Falk, Courtney. *Gray hat hacking: Morally black and white.* CERIAS Technical Report, 2004--20), Lafayette, IN: Center for Education and Research in Information Assurance and Security, Purdue University, 2014.

Fenrich, Kim. "Securing your control system: the" CIA triad" is a widely used benchmark for evaluating information system security effectiveness." *Power Engineering* 112, no. 2 (2008): 44-49.

Ferrag, Mohamed Amine, Leandros A. Maglaras, Helge Janicke, and Jianmin Jiang. "A survey on privacy-preserving schemes for smart grid communications." *arXiv preprint arXiv:1611.07722* (2016).

Finlayson, Ross, Timothy Mann, Jeffrey Mogul, and Marvin Theimer. "A reverse address resolution protocol." (1984).

Fonseca, Jose, Marco Vieira, and Henrique Madeira. "Testing and comparing web vulnerability scanning tools for SQL injection and XSS attacks." In *13th Pacific Rim international symposium on dependable computing (PRDC 2007)*, pp. 365-372. IEEE, 2007.

Forouzan, Behrouz A. *Cryptography & network security.* McGraw-Hill, Inc., 2007.

Fovino, Igor Nai, Luca Guidi, Marcelo Masera, and Alberto Stefanini. "Cybersecurity assessment of a power plant." *Electric Power Systems Research* 81, no. 2 (2011): 518-526.

Furnell, S. M., M. Gennatou, and P. S. Dowland. "A prototype tool for information security awareness and training." *Logistics Information Management* 15, no. 5/6 (2002): 352-357.

Furnell, Steven. "Hackers, viruses and malicious software." *Handbook of internet crime* (2010): 173-193.

Garera, Sujata, Niels Provos, Monica Chew, and Aviel D. Rubin. "A framework for detection and measurement of phishing attacks." In *Proceedings of the 2007 ACM workshop on Recurring malcode*, pp. 1-8. ACM, 2007.

Gharibi, Wajeb, and Maha Shaabi. "Cyber threats in social networking websites." *arXiv preprint arXiv:1202.2420* (2012).

Goddard, Michelle. "The EU General Data Protection Regulation (GDPR): European regulation that has a global impact." *International Journal of Market Research* 59, no. 6 (2017): 703-705.

Goel, Ashish, Prerana Gupta Poddar, and Monika Agrawal. "Two new phase sequence sets for PAPR reduction in SLM-OFDM systems without side information." In *Proceedings of the 1st International Conference on Wireless Technologies for Humanitarian Relief*, pp. 35-40. ACM, 2011.

Gómez, Antonio F., Gregorio Martínez, and Óscar Cánovas. "New security services based on PKI." *Future Generation Computer Systems* 19, no. 2 (2003): 251-262.

Gulwani, Sumit, William R. Harris, and Rishabh Singh. "Spreadsheet data manipulation using examples." *Communications of the ACM* 55, no. 8 (2012): 97-105.

Gupta, Satinder Bal, and Aditya Mittal. *Introduction to Database Management System.* Laxmi Publications, Ltd., 2009.

Gupta, Shashank, and Brij Bhooshan Gupta. "Cross-Site Scripting (XSS) attacks and defense mechanisms: classification and state-of-the-art." *International Journal of System Assurance Engineering and Management* 8, no. 1 (2017): 512-530.

Halfond, William G., Jeremy Viegas, and Alessandro Orso. "A classification of SQL-injection attacks and countermeasures." In *Proceedings of the IEEE International Symposium on Secure Software Engineering*, vol. 1, pp. 13-15. IEEE, 2006.

Harper, Allen, Shon Harris, Jonathan Ness, Chris Eagle, Gideon Lenkey, and Terron Williams. *Gray hat hacking the ethical hackers handbook.* McGraw-Hill Osborne Media, 2011.

Hauben, Michael. "History of ARPANET." *Site de l'Instituto Superior de Engenharia do Porto* 17 (2007).

Holostov, Vladimir, Thomas W. Kuehnel, Shai Guday, Naile Daoud, and Tript Singh Lamba. "Service-assisted network access point selection." U.S. Patent 8,665,847, issued March 4, 2014.

Housley, R., J. Curran, G. Huston, and D. Conrad. "The internet numbers registry system." *RFC 7020 (Informational), Internet Engineering Task Force* (2013).

Jeske, Tobias. "Floating car data from smartphones: What google and waze know about you and how hackers can control traffic." *Proc. of the BlackHat Europe* (2013): 1-12.

Kaminsky, Dan. "Explorations in namespace: white-hat hacking across the domain name system." *Communications of the ACM* 49, no. 6 (2006): 62-69.

Kandukuri, Balachandra Reddy, and Atanu Rakshit. "Cloud security issues." In *2009 IEEE International Conference on Services Computing*, pp. 517-520. IEEE, 2009.

Kang, Jerry. "Trojan horses of race." *Harv. L. Rev.* 118 (2004): 1489.

Khan, Muhammad Salman, Ken Ferens, and Witold Kinsner. "A chaotic complexity measure for cognitive machine classification of cyber-attacks on computer networks." *International Journal of Cognitive Informatics and Natural Intelligence (IJCINI)* 8, no. 3 (2014): 45-69.

Khansa, Lara, and Christopher W. Zobel. "Assessing innovations in cloud security." *Journal of Computer Information Systems* 54, no. 3 (2014): 45-56.

Kiesler, Sara, Robert Kraut, Jonathon Cummings, Bonka Boneva, Vicki Helgeson, and Anne Crawford. "Internet evolution and social impact." *It & Society* 1, no. 1 (2002): 120-134.

King, John Leslie, Rebecca E. Grinter, and Jeanne M. Pickering. "The rise and fall of

Knapp, Eric D., and Joel Thomas Langill. *Industrial Network Security: Securing critical infrastructure networks for smart grid, SCADA, and other Industrial Control Systems*. Syngress, 2014.

Kshetri, Nir. "Pattern of global cyber war and crime: A conceptual framework." *Journal of International Management* 11, no. 4 (2005): 541-562.

Kumar, Sanjeev. "Smurf-based distributed denial of service (ddos) attack amplification in internet." In *Second International Conference on Internet Monitoring and Protection (ICIMP 2007)*, pp. 25-25. IEEE, 2007.

Lambrinoudakis, Costas, Stefanos Gritzalis, Fredj Dridi, and GüNther Pernul. "Security requirements for e-government services: a methodological approach for developing a common PKI-based security policy." *Computer Communications* 26, no. 16 (2003): 1873-1883.

Leiner, Barry M., Vinton G. Cerf, David D. Clark, Robert E. Kahn, Leonard Kleinrock, Daniel C. Lynch, Jon Postel, Larry G. Roberts, and Stephen Wolff. "A brief history of the Internet." *ACM SIGCOMM Computer Communication Review* 39, no. 5 (2009): 22-31.

Liang, Jinjin, Jian Jiang, Haixin Duan, Kang Li, and Jianping Wu. "Measuring query latency of top level DNS servers." In *International Conference on Passive and Active Network Measurement*, pp. 145-154. Springer, Berlin, Heidelberg, 2013.

Lopez, Igor, and Marina Aguado. "Cybersecurity analysis of the european train control system." *IEEE Communications Magazine* 53, no. 10 (2015): 110-116.

Luallen, Matthew. "Breaches on the rise in control systems: A sans survey." *Retrieved February* 24 (2014): 2015.

Lukasik, Stephen. "Why the ARPANET was built." *IEEE Annals of the History of Computing* 33, no. 3 (2010): 4-21.

Lusthaus, Jonathan. "How organised is organised cybercrime?." *Global Crime* 14, no. 1 (2013): 52-60.

Lyon, Gordon Fyodor. *Nmap network scanning: The official Nmap project guide to network discovery and security scanning.* Insecure, 2009.

Lyu, Michael R., and Lorrien KY Lau. "Firewall security: Policies, testing and performance evaluation." In *Proceedings 24th Annual International Computer Software and Applications Conference. COMPSAC2000*, pp. 116-121. IEEE, 2000.

Maglaras, Leandros A., Jianmin Jiang, and Tiago J. Cruz. "Combining ensemble methods and social network metrics for improving accuracy of OCSVM on intrusion detection in SCADA systems." *Journal of Information Security and Applications* 30 (2016): 15-26.

Mahmoud, Rwan, Tasneem Yousuf, Fadi Aloul, and Imran Zualkernan. "Internet of things (IoT) security: Current status, challenges and prospective measures." In *2015 10th International Conference for Internet Technology and Secured Transactions (ICITST)*, pp. 336-341. IEEE, 2015.

Manky, Derek. "Cybercrime as a service: a very modern business." *Computer Fraud & Security* 2013, no. 6 (2013): 9-13.

McCusker, Rob. "Transnational organised cyber crime: distinguishing threat from reality." *Crime, law and social change* 46, no. 4-5 (2006): 257-273.

McGraw, Gary. "Software security." *IEEE Security & Privacy* 2, no. 2 (2004): 80-83.

McMillan, Robert. "Siemens: Stuxnet worm hit industrial systems." *Computerworld* 14 (2010).

Meier, J. D., Alex Mackman, Michael Dunner, Srinath Vasireddy, Ray Escamilla, and Anandha Murukan. *Improving web application security: threats and countermeasures*. Vol. 3. Redmond: Microsoft Corporation, 2003.

Metso, Janne. "Penetration Testing: Ethical Hacking." (2019).

Mirkovic, Jelena, Sven Dietrich, David Dittrich, and Peter Reiher. *Internet denial of service: attack and defense mechanisms (Radia Perlman Computer Networking and Security)*. Prentice Hall PTR, 2004.

Mitchell, Robert, and Ing-Ray Chen. "A survey of intrusion detection techniques for cyber-physical systems." *ACM Computing Surveys (CSUR)* 46, no. 4 (2014): 55.

Mukkamala, Srinivas, Andrew Sung, and Ajith Abraham. "Cybersecurity challenges: Designing efficient intrusion detection systems and antivirus tools." *Vemuri, V. Rao, Enhancing Computer Security with Smart Technology.(Auerbach, 2006)* (2005): 125-163.

Naedele, Martin. "Addressing IT security for critical control systems." In *2007 40th Annual Hawaii International*

Conference on System Sciences (HICSS'07), pp. 115-115. IEEE, 2007.

Nagarajan, Ajay, Jan M. Allbeck, Arun Sood, and Terry L. Janssen. "Exploring game design for cybersecurity training." In *2012 IEEE International Conference on Cyber Technology in Automation, Control, and Intelligent Systems (CYBER)*, pp. 256-262. IEEE, 2012.

Nash, Andrew, William Duane, Celia Joseph, Derek Brink, and Bill Duane. *PKI: Implementing and Managing E-security.* Berkeley, California: Osborne/McGraw-Hill, 2001.

Nazir, Sajid, Shushma Patel, and Dilip Patel. "Assessing and augmenting SCADA cybersecurity: A survey of techniques." *Computers & Security* 70 (2017): 436-454.

Ngo, Fawn T., and Raymond Paternoster. "Cybercrime Victimization: An examination of Individual and Situational level factors." *International Journal of Cyber Criminology* 5, no. 1 (2011).

Nicholson, Andrew, Tim Watson, Peter Norris, Alistair Duffy, and Roy Isbell. "A taxonomy of technical attribution techniques for cyber attacks." In *European Conference on Information Warfare and Security*, p. 188. Academic Conferences International Limited, 2012.

Nykodym, Nick, Robert Taylor, and Julia Vilela. "Criminal profiling and insider cyber crime." *Computer Law & Security Review* 21, no. 5 (2005): 408-414.

Nykodym, Nick, Sonny Ariss, and Katarina Kurtz. "Computer addiction and cyber crime." *Journal of Leadership, Accountability and Ethics* (2008): 78.

Oberheide, Jon, Evan Cooke, and Farnam Jahanian. "CloudAV: N-Version Antivirus in the Network Cloud." In *USENIX Security Symposium*, pp. 91-106. 2008.

Oliver, Jonathan J., and David A. Koblas. "Message classification based on likelihood of spoofing." U.S. Patent 8,856,239, issued October 7, 2014.

Palmer, Charles C. "Ethical hacking." *IBM Systems Journal* 40, no. 3 (2001): 769-780.

Pan, Shengyi, Thomas Morris, and Uttam Adhikari. "Classification of disturbances and cyber-attacks in power systems using heterogeneous time-synchronized data." *IEEE Transactions on Industrial Informatics* 11, no. 3 (2015): 650-662.

Pardridge, William M. "Drug and gene targeting to the brain with molecular Trojan horses." *Nature reviews Drug discovery* 1, no. 2 (2002): 131.

Park, Heum, SunHo Cho, and Hyuk-Chul Kwon. "Cyber forensics ontology for cyber criminal investigation." In *International Conference on Forensics in Telecommunications, Information, and Multimedia*, pp. 160-165. Springer, Berlin, Heidelberg, 2009.

Pauna, Adrian, Konstantinos Moulinos, Matina Lakka, J. May, and T. Tryfonas. "Can we learn from SCADA security incidents." *White Paper, European Union Agency for*

Network and Information Security, Heraklion, Crete, Greece (2013).

Payton, Anne. "Determining the proper response to online extortion." In *Proceedings of the 2nd annual conference on Information security curriculum development*, pp. 122-126. ACM, 2005.

Perrig, Adrian, John Stankovic, and David Wagner. "Security in wireless sensor networks." (2004): 53-57.

Perrin, Chad. "The CIA triad." *Dostopno na: http://www. techrepublic. com/blog/security/the-cia-triad/488* (2008).

Pike, Ronald E. "The "ethics" of teaching ethical hacking." *Journal of International Technology and Information Management* 22, no. 4 (2013): 4.

Pinkas, Benny, and Tomas Sander. "Securing passwords against dictionary attacks." In *Proceedings of the 9th ACM conference on Computer and communications security*, pp. 161-170. ACM, 2002.

Poe, Marshall T. *A History of Communications: Media and Society from the Evolution of Speech to the Internet*. Cambridge University Press, 2010.

Postel, Jon. "Domain name system structure and delegation." (1994).

Pouzin, Louis. "Presentation and major design aspects of the CYCLADES computer network." In *Proceedings of the third ACM symposium on Data communications and Data networks: Analysis and design*, pp. 80-87. ACM, 1973.

Probst, Christian W., Jeffrey Hunker, Matt Bishop, and Dieter Gollmann, eds. *Insider threats in cybersecurity*. Vol. 49. Springer Science & Business Media, 2010.

Radianti, Jaziar, and Jose J. Gonzalez. "Understanding hidden information security threats: The vulnerability black market." In *2007 40th Annual Hawaii International Conference on System Sciences (HICSS'07)*, pp. 156c-156c. IEEE, 2007.

Radianti, Jaziar, Eliot Rich, and Jose J. Gonzalez. "Vulnerability black markets: Empirical evidence and scenario simulation." In *2009 42nd Hawaii International Conference on System Sciences*, pp. 1-10. IEEE, 2009.

Ralston, Patricia AS, James H. Graham, and Jefferey L. Hieb. "Cybersecurity risk assessment for SCADA and DCS networks." *ISA transactions* 46, no. 4 (2007): 583-594.

Ramgovind, Sumant, Mariki M. Eloff, and Elme Smith. "The management of security in cloud computing." In *2010 Information Security for South Africa*, pp. 1-7. IEEE, 2010.

Rantala, Ramona R. "Cybercrime against businesses, 2005." *organization* 15, no. 14 (2008): 9.

Rantala, Ramona R. *Cybercrime against businesses*. US Department of Justice, Office of Justice Programs, Bureau of Justice Statistics, 2004.

Rashid, Awais, Rajiv Ramdhany, Matthew Edwards, Sarah Kibirige Mukisa, Muhammad Ali Babar, David Hutchison, and Ruzanna Chitchyan. "Detecting and preventing data exfiltration." (2014).

Rastogi, Vaibhav, Yan Chen, and William Enck. "AppsPlayground: automatic security analysis of smartphone applications." In *Proceedings of the third ACM conference on Data and application security and privacy*, pp. 209-220. ACM, 2013.

Regalado, Daniel, Shon Harris, Allen Harper, Chris Eagle, Jonathan Ness, Branko Spasojevic, Ryan Linn, and Stephen Sims. *Gray Hat Hacking: The Ethical Hacker's Handbook*. New York: McGraw-Hill Education, 2015.

Roelker, Daniel. "HTTP IDS evasions revisited." *Sourcefire Inc* (2003).

Rogel, Lawrence S. "Preventing malware attacks in virtualized mobile devices." U.S. Patent 8,341,749, issued December 25, 2012.

Ronaldson, Nicholas. "HACKING: THE NAKED AGE CYBERCRIME, CLAPPER & STANDING, AND THE DEBATE BETWEEN STATE AND FEDERAL DATA BREACH NOTIFICATION LAWS." Northwestern Journal of Technology and Intellectual Property 16, no. 4 (2019): 305.

Roscini, Marco. *Cyber operations and the use of force in international law*. Oxford University Press, USA, 2014.

Roy, Arpan, Dong Seong Kim, and Kishor S. Trivedi. "Cybersecurity analysis using attack countermeasure trees." In *Proceedings of the Sixth Annual Workshop on Cybersecurity and Information Intelligence Research*, p. 28. ACM, 2010.

Ryoo, Jungwoo, Syed Rizvi, William Aiken, and John Kissell. "Cloud security auditing: challenges and emerging approaches." *IEEE Security & Privacy* 12, no. 6 (2013): 68-74.

Saini, Hemraj, Yerra Shankar Rao, and Tarini Charan Panda. "Cyber-crimes and their impacts: A review." *International Journal of Engineering Research and Applications* 2, no. 2 (2012): 202-209.

Schell, Bernadette Hlubik, and Clemens Martin. *Cybercrime: A reference handbook*. ABC-CLIO, 2004.

Schieferdecker, Ina, Juergen Grossmann, and Martin Schneider. "Model-based security testing." *arXiv preprint arXiv:1202.6118* (2012).

Schjolberg, Stein. *The History of Cybercrime: 1976-2014*. BoD–Books on Demand, 2014.

Schmitt, Michael N., ed. *Tallinn manual on the international law applicable to cyber warfare*. Cambridge University Press, 2013.

Schmitt, Michael. "Classification of cyber conflict." *Journal of conflict and security law* 17, no. 2 (2012): 245-260.

Segal, Ben. "A short history of Internet protocols at CERN." *Professional webpage. April. http://ben. home. cern. ch/ben/TCPHIST. html* (1995).

Seitz, Justin. *Gray Hat Python: Python programming for hackers and reverse engineers*. no starch press, 2009.

Shaikh, Farhan Bashir, and Sajjad Haider. "Security threats in cloud computing." In *2011 International Conference for Internet Technology and Secured Transactions*, pp. 214-219. IEEE, 2011.

Shariff, Shaheen, and Leanne Johnny. "Cyber-libel and cyber-bullying: Can schools protect student reputations and free-expression in virtual environments?." *Education Law Journal* 16, no. 3 (2007): 307.

Sheridan, Lorraine P., and Tim Grant. "Is cyberstalking different?." *Psychology, crime & law* 13, no. 6 (2007): 627-640.

Shostack, Adam. "Elevation of privilege: Drawing developers into threat modeling." In *2014 {USENIX} Summit on Gaming, Games, and Gamification in Security Education (3GSE 14)*. 2014.

Shukla, Sandeep K. "Cybersecurity of cyber physical systems: Cyber threats and defense of critical infrastructures." In *2016 29th International Conference on VLSI Design and 2016 15th International Conference on Embedded Systems (VLSID)*, pp. 30-31. IEEE, 2016.

Singh, Talwant. "Cyber law & information technology." *District & Sessions Judge, Delhi* (2007).

Sinha, Prosenjit, Amine Boukhtouta, Victor Heber Belarde, and Mourad Debbabi. "Insights from the Analysis of the Mariposa Botnet." In *2010 Fifth International Conference on Risks and Security of Internet and Systems (CRiSIS)*, pp. 1-9. IEEE, 2010.

Smith, Russell, Peter Grabosky, and Gregor Urbas. "Cyber criminals on trial." *Criminal Justice Matters* 58, no. 1 (2004): 22-23.

Snail, Sizwe. "Cyber Crime in South Africa–Hacking, cracking, and other unlawful online activities." *Journal of Information, Law and Technology* 1 (2009): 2009-1.

Spitzberg, Brian H., and Gregory Hoobler. "Cyberstalking and the technologies of interpersonal terrorism." *New media & society* 4, no. 1 (2002): 71-92.

Srinivas, Sethuraman, and Archana Nair. "Security maturity in NoSQL databases-are they secure enough to haul the modern it applications?." In *2015 International Conference on Advances in Computing, Communications and Informatics (ICACCI)*, pp. 739-744. IEEE, 2015.

Stallings, William. *Cryptography and Network Security, 4/E*. Pearson Education India, 2006.

Stallings, William. *Network and internetwork security: principles and practice*. Vol. 1. Englewood Cliffs, NJ: Prentice Hall, 1995.

Stoica, Ion, Daniel Adkins, Shelley Zhuang, Scott Shenker, and Sonesh Surana. "Internet indirection infrastructure." In *ACM SIGCOMM Computer Communication Review*, vol. 32, no. 4, pp. 73-86. ACM, 2002.

Sullivan, Bryan. "Preventing a brute force or dictionary attack: how to keep the brutes away from your loot." *Pridobljeno (17.4. 2014) iz CODE Project: http://www. codeproject.*

com/Articles/17111/Preventing-a-Brute-Force-or-Dictionary-Attack-How* (2007).

Szor, Peter. The Art of Computer Virus Research and Defense: ART COMP VIRUS RES DEFENSE _p1. Pearson Education, 2005.

Taylor, Robert W., Eric J. Fritsch, and John Liederbach. *Digital crime and digital terrorism*. Prentice Hall Press, 2014.

Tian-yang, Gu, Shi Yin-Sheng, and Fang You-yuan. "Research on software security testing." *World Academy of science, engineering and Technology* 70 (2010): 647-651.

Tyree, David. "Scripted distributed denial-of-service (DDoS) attack discrimination using turing tests." U.S. Patent Application 09/793,733, filed August 29, 2002.

Tzokatziou, Grigoris, Leandros Maglaras, and Helge Janicke. "Insecure by design: using human interface devices to exploit SCADA systems." In *Proceedings of the 3rd International Symposium for ICS & SCADA Cybersecurity Research*, pp. 103-106. BCS Learning & Development Ltd., 2015.

Uma, M., and Ganapathi Padmavathi. "A Survey on Various Cyber Attacks and their Classification." *IJ Network Security* 15, no. 5 (2013): 390-396.

Umanailo, M. Chairul Basrun, Imam Fachruddin, Deviana Mayasari, Rudy Kurniawan, Dewien Nabielah Agustin, Rini Ganefwati, Pardamean Daulay et al. "Cybercrime Case as Impact Development of Communication Technology That

Troubling Society." *Int. J. Sci. Technol. Res* 8, no. 9 (2019): 1224-1228.

Vaithianathasamy, Swami. "AI vs AI: fraudsters turn defensive technology into an attack tool." *Computer Fraud & Security* 2019, no. 8 (2019): 6-8.

Vixie, Paul, Susan Thomson, Yakov Rekhter, and Jim Bound. *Dynamic updates in the domain name system (DNS UPDATE)*. RFC 2136, April, 1997.

Vogt, Philipp, Florian Nentwich, Nenad Jovanovic, Engin Kirda, Christopher Kruegel, and Giovanni Vigna. "Cross Site Scripting Prevention with Dynamic Data Tainting and Static Analysis." In *NDSS*, vol. 2007, p. 12. 2007.

Voigt, Paul, and Axel Von dem Bussche. "The eu general data protection regulation (gdpr)." *A Practical Guide, 1st Ed., Cham: Springer International Publishing* (2017).

Vykopal, Jan. "A flow-level taxonomy and prevalence of brute force attacks." In *International Conference on Advances in Computing and Communications*, pp. 666-675. Springer, Berlin, Heidelberg, 2011.

Waldman, Barry J. "A Unified Approach to Cyber-Libel: Defamation on the Internet, a Suggested Approach." *Richmond Journal of Law & Technology* 6, no. 2 (1999): 9.

Wang, Xueqiang, Kun Sun, Yuewu Wang, and Jiwu Jing. "DeepDroid: Dynamically Enforcing Enterprise Policy on Android Devices." In Ndss. 2015.

Wasik, Martin. "Computers and the blackmail threat." *Computer Law & Security Review* 5, no. 4 (1989): 22-23.

Wei, Kei, Muthusrinivasan Muthuprasanna, and Suraj Kothari. "Preventing SQL injection attacks in stored procedures." In *Australian Software Engineering Conference (ASWEC'06)*, pp. 8-pp. IEEE, 2006.

Williams, Matthew. *Virtually criminal: Crime, deviance and regulation online*. Routledge, 2006.

Willison, Robert, and Mikko Siponen. "Overcoming the insider: reducing employee computer crime through Situational Crime Prevention." *Communications of the ACM* 52, no. 9 (2009): 133-137.

Wilson, Mark, and Joan Hash. "Building an information technology security awareness and training program." *NIST Special publication* 800, no. 50 (2003): 1-39.

Wilson, Stephen. "The importance of PKI today." *China Communications* (2005): 15.

Wood, Andy, Ying He, Leandros Maglaras, and Helge Janicke. "An architectural security pattern for risk management of industry control systems within critical national infrastructure." (2017).

Wood, Anthony D., and John A. Stankovic. "Denial of service in sensor networks." *computer* 35, no. 10 (2002): 54-62.

Wood, Lori A. "Cyber-Defamation and the Single Publication Rule." *BUL Rev.* 81 (2001): 895.

Wu, Min, Robert C. Miller, and Simson L. Garfinkel. "Do security toolbars actually prevent phishing attacks?." In *Proceedings of the SIGCHI conference on Human Factors in computing systems*, pp. 601-610. ACM, 2006.

Yoder, Joseph, and Jeffrey Barcalow. "Architectural patterns for enabling application security." In *Proceedings of the 4th Conference on Patterns Language of Programming (PLoP'97)*, vol. 2. 1997.

Young, Randall, Lixuan Zhang, and Victor R. Prybutok. "Hacking into the minds of hackers." *Information Systems Management* 24, no. 4 (2007): 281-287.

Zargar, Saman Taghavi, James Joshi, and David Tipper. "A survey of defense mechanisms against distributed denial of service (DDoS) flooding attacks." *IEEE communications surveys & tutorials* 15, no. 4 (2013): 2046-2069.

Zhang, Zhanjun, Yong Li, and Zhong-xiao Man. "Improved Wojcik's eavesdropping attack on ping-pong protocol without eavesdropping-induced channel loss." *Physics Letters A* 341, no. 5-6 (2005): 385-389.

Zhang, Zhanjun, Zhongxiao Man, and Yong Li. "Improving Wójcik's eavesdropping attack on the ping–pong protocol." *Physics Letters A* 333, no. 1-2 (2004): 46-50.

Zhao, Kai, and Lina Ge. "A survey on the internet of things security." In *2013 Ninth international conference on computational intelligence and security*, pp. 663-667. IEEE, 2013.

Zhao, Mingyi, Jens Grossklags, and Kai Chen. "An exploratory study of white hat behaviors in a web vulnerability disclosure program." In *Proceedings of the 2014 ACM workshop on security information workers*, pp. 51-58. ACM, 2014.

Zhu, Bonnie, Anthony Joseph, and Shankar Sastry. "A taxonomy of cyber attacks on SCADA systems." In *2011 International conference on internet of things and 4th international conference on cyber, physical and social computing*, pp. 380-388. IEEE, 2011.

Zitser, Misha, Richard Lippmann, and Tim Leek. "Testing static analysis tools using exploitable buffer overflows from open source code." In *ACM SIGSOFT Software Engineering Notes*, vol. 29, no. 6, pp. 97-106. ACM, 2004.